# ANDEAN AWAKENING

# ANDEAN AWAKENING

## An Inca Guide to Mystical Peru

## Jorge Luis Delgado
with MaryAnn Male, PhD

Council Oak Books
San Francisco / Tulsa

Council Oak Books, LLC
counciloakbooks.com

Published 2006
Printed in Canada

Cover and interior design by Carl Brune

Cover and interior photography by Theron Male, PhD
Photographs of Aramu Muru's Doorway on page 90 courtesy of
Christine LaBang

Library of Congress Cataloging-in-Publication Data
Delgado, Jorge Luis.
    Andean awakening : An Inca guide to mystical Peru / Jorge Luis
Delgado with MaryAnn Male.
        p. cm.
    ISBN-13: 978-1-57178-193-2
    ISBN-10: 1-57178-193-5
1. Inca cosmology. 2. Incas--Religion. 3. Incas--Rites and ceremonies.
4. Quero cosmology. 5. Quero Indians--Religion. 6. Quero Indians--Rites
and ceremonies. 7. Shamanism--Andes Region. 8. Medicine, Magic,
mystic, and spagiric--Andes Region. 9. New Age movement--Andes
Region. I. Male, MaryAnn. II. Title.
    F3429.3.R3D43 2006
    299.8'8324--dc22
                                                            2006005430

*With so much love to the Cosmic Family, to the Father Sun, to the Pachamama, to the Apukunas, to my innumerable teachers, to my mother, Margarita, to my father, Carlos Ricardo, to my brothers and sisters. To my wife, Dionny, to my daughters, Claudia and Amara , to my sons, Juan Rodrigo and Georgio and to all the people who helped me with this offering of love. To Theron and MaryAnn, my Eagle Family from the North who fly together with me and the Condor of the South. And to you, for absorbing this offering.*

JORGE LUIS

*Theron and I are grateful to our special teacher Clem Tamborino, and in memory of Terri Ross. We appreciate the love and support of our family, Kay Magee, Eileen and Jim Stec, T.J. and Tracy Male, Heather Male, Jack and Susan Owens, and our inspirations, Katie, Karly, Jason and Lauren.*

MARYANN MALE

# Contents

Foreword       xi
*David Morehouse, PhD*

Introduction       1

Aramu Muru's Doorway       5
The Dream ~ Inca Tunuhwire ~ Copamaya ~Three Teenagers ~ Bebedero del Inca ~ Reading the Stones ~ City of Spirits ~ The Discovery ~ Arrival of PachaKuti ~ Path of the Chacaruna

Aymara Heritage       19
Cholla ~ Healing the Babies ~ Puno ~ Mysterious Lady ~ Unexpected Ceremony ~ Pre-Incan to Incan Heritage ~ Interest Grows ~ Madonna of the Lake ~ Sacred Lake ~ Ignoring the Heritage

Visiting Crystal       33
Birthplace of the Incas ~ Encounter with the Crystal ~ An Antenna ~ Becoming a Believer ~ Sillustani ~ "All Gods and New Faces" ~ Not on Tuesday ~ Reed Islands ~ Ruben Cederño ~ Condori

Dancing Fire People       49
Antonio ~ Community Life ~ Pacha ~ Chewing the Coca Leaves ~Uku Pacha ~ Kay Pacha ~ Hanan Pacha ~ The Condor Soars ~ Office Blessing ~ The Initiation

Elders from the Mountains       65
Cusi Pata ~ Mariano ~ The Bumpy Road ~ The Village ~Trial Marriage ~ Apukunas - "Take It Away" ~ Preparing the Mesa ~ Calling the Apus ~ Words of Preparation ~ The Ceremony

## High Plateau 99

Cutimbo ~ Temples Amid the Crops ~ Transcendental Pumas ~ Mountain Cara Cara~ Lupaka People ~ Amantani ~ Island Boat Ride ~ Temples and Chincanas~ All That Glitters ~ UFO Sighting

## Charazani Healer 115

Mountain Village ~ Flags ~ Donkey Dispute ~ Hummingbird vs. Condor ~ Struck by Lightning ~ Reading the Future ~ Herbal Remedies ~Twelve Dishes ~ Herbs ~ Amulets and Talismans

## Sacred Valley of the Incas 129

Solar Expressions ~ Don Miguel's Visit ~ Urco ~ Pisac ~ Fire Ceremony ~ Ollantaytambo ~ Moray ~ Cusco ~ Golden Disk ~ Vibrant Marketplace ~ Tipon ~ Tupananchiscama

## Three Laws Revealed 145

Arms of Pachamama ~ Connecting to the Golden Disk ~ Three Worlds ~ Becoming the Inca ~ Munay ~ Llancay ~ Yachay ~ High Priest ~ Testing the Fear ~ Back in the Moment ~ Seeking Wisdom ~ Endings and Beginnings

## Epilogue 167

| | |
|---|---|
| Author's Note | 169 |
| Apus | 169 |
| Glossary | 171 |
| Index | 175 |

## Acknowledgements

*Our special thanks to our readers and supporters: Rita Rivera, Alan Hardman, John Buzenberg, Bontia Luz, Ivan Salas, Rosario Rojas, Broz Tito, Romel Sanizo (designer of the maps), Don Pedro Alarcón, Paulette Millichap, Frank Hayhurst, Andrea Mikana and Mark, Joyce Kadwell, Hinda Bornstein, Patty DiGiacomo, Alex Goldwater, Peggie Federico, Susan Magee and Beth Goldner.*

# FOREWORD

## David Morehouse, PhD

n 1987, I was serving as a United States Army Ranger Company Commander, training Jordanian Rangers in their desert kingdom. During a dangerous live fire exercise, I was struck in the head and knocked unconscious by a stray machine gun bullet. The experience ushered me violently into another world. It was here, in this altered state, that my life journey began anew. What I learned on that day about the world, about other worlds, other civilizations and our connection to them set into motion a series of events leading to a new identity, one quite different from my present one. The months and years that followed were guided by information, often not solely mined from this world, which led to decisions drastically altering my life. In short, an eighteen-year military career ended, and a life of teaching began. Through this teaching I met my dear friends Theron and MaryAnn Male, who over the next five years spoke to me in an inspired manner about a man who "walks in many worlds," a man "who will know the place where your transformation began." The man of whom they spoke was Jorge Luis Delgado.

Years passed, during which I kept hearing of this great man of vision and spirit, a teacher and guide leading beings from this physical world on a path seeking truth, finding knowledge, and attaining wisdom. A man who with blessed voice and gracious heart opened doorways for all who traveled with him. A man who loved life and taught the old ways blended with a modern manner and sensibility. A man with a heart a grand as the Andes and a sense of humor as broad as the sea. I heard of this man, but I did not meet him until May 2004, when Theron and MaryAnn finally managed to bring the two of us together in Peru.

I make no pretense of being a spiritual man; however, I know one when I see one. I make no pretense of enlightenment, of walking in worlds, the physical, and the non-physical; nonetheless, I know it when I see it. On that brilliant sunny day in Juliaca, Peru, while still reeling from the altitude and long days of travel, my eyes fell upon a man whose countenance was indeed a portrait of his soul. His eyes completely marked his intentions, and they were pure. It was clear to my heart, in that moment, that this man had been prepared by something outside of himself, that his life had been shifted for a reason that even he did not fully understand, and because of it, his life could never be the same again. Jorge Luis Delgado was chosen, and in that instant, I knew it. I was overtaken by a desire to know this man, to learn from him, to ask him and know that the answers given would not be solely of this world. I was in the presence of a "chacaruna," a living guide who had been to the other side of the moment, into the quantum world of infinite possibility, into the realm of the un-manifested, a man who was given the task to bridge existences and to prepare those who would walk these bridges with knowledge and courage.

In an instant, a friendship was born, or as Jorge Luis would say, "We found one another again." I spent several weeks with Jorge that year and another series of weeks the following year, each time progressing deeper into my understanding of the spiritual history of humanity and the potential now welling within the human condition for promise and possibility, for transformation and growth. It was with Jorge Luis that I validated my understanding that each of us has the power to connect to the Divine, the Cosmos, the Pacha. It was with Jorge Luis that I learned to travel yet another way, through special ceremonies and initiations, helping my students and me to connect to the Spirit world as well as to our spiritual selves. I am forever grateful to Jorge for his teaching, his example, and for his life in the service of others.

It is a great honor and privilege for me to write this foreword to Jorge Luis's first, but certainly not last, book. I know that many books will follow, that a life of teaching and gaining wisdom cannot be bound between the pages of just one book, yet this work is beautifully done, complete, and inspiring. Upon finishing it, you will know more than you imagined possible about the mysticism of Peru, the history, the magic, the place, the people, and you will read it as though it were the first time you had ever heard it because the voice is fresh, pure and true, and inspired by the illumination of personal experience. As you read, you will come to know Jorge Luis, and you too will want to share in his wisdom and walk with him in the ancient land of the Inca, to be lead across the bridge to other worlds, to other beings, and to new understandings of why you are here and where you are going. You will transform your present understanding of purpose, expanding it to new horizons, reaching to the edge of knowledge and beyond. My friends, enjoy the journey inward that this heroic work delivers.

**Major David Morehouse, PhD,** is a highly decorated former US Special Operations officer and Army Ranger Company Commander. His work is critically endorsed by Anthony Robbins, Don Miguel Ruiz, and Deepak Chopra. In 1987, he was struck in the head by a stray Jordanian machine gun bullet; the wound opened him to a series of visions and dreams of realms beyond the physical. Dr. Morehouse left the tactical community with a new awareness of the world around him and beyond. In 1996, Dr. Morehouse resigned his commission and became the premiere trainer of the art and science of remote viewing. He has trained over twenty thousand students globally, and his book, *Psychic Warrior*, is published in 16 languages.

# INTRODUCTION
## Jorge Luis Delgado, Puno, Peru

On a clear night in early May in the Peruvian mountains 14,000 feet above sea level, the heavens are crowded with visible stars. Yet, the "Southern Cross" dominates the sky. The "Eye of the Llama," a black cloud in the middle of the Milky Way, flies toward the Southern Cross. Its "eyes" are the stars Alpha and Beta. The "llama" stretches its long neck and tucks its front legs inward in a gesture of reverence. On the third of May, the Southern Cross is at its zenith in the sky, and the Festival of the Cross is celebrated with all-night fiestas in the mountain villages of Peru, as it has been for centuries from pre-Incan times. Since the time of the Spaniards, the feast has also been used to celebrate the Holy Cross of the Catholic Church. Almost every night in May the priests go to a different mountain village and celebrate Mass at a permanent white cross atop the local mountain.

This festival of the Southern Cross is a pre-Incan and Incan tradition, still very significant in the lives of the people. In the Inca mind, there is no separation of the physical and the spiritual life of the people. When the Incas gaze at the Southern Cross, they see a "bridge" to go from one side of the Milky Way to the other side of the Milky Way. It is a point of departure during this lifetime for the spirit and also a point of transition into the next life. So there are many celebrations in the Andean communities each year from May to August.

Musicians with Andean panpipes and drums play for hours while the people dance all of the day and night. There is food and drink everywhere, and the children dance until they fall asleep. The "llama" in the sky watches over all of the festivities. This "llama" has watched over my country for many, many thousands of years. Let me tell you a little about my most beautiful country. Peru lies on the west coast of South America on the coast of the Pacific Ocean. It is bordered on the north by Equador and Columbia and by Brazil and Bolivia in the east. Chile lies to the south. There are three main regions with desert-like qualities along the coast, the magnificent Andes Mountains and the altiplano in the center, and the jungle in the east.

Almost half of the population is indigenous, or descendants of the Incas, and live mainly in the central region. Many others are Spanish or a mixture of heritages. As far back as the pre-Inca cultures, the regions traded their specialties and goods. The Inca "conquerors," according to legend, were accepted because they improved the organization of trade and the farming techniques of the people. Quechua and Aymara had been spoken in the highlands of the Andes for a couple of hundred years before what is called the Inca Empire flourished in the 15<sup>th</sup> century. The Spanish arrived in the 1530s and established their rule by 1542. Despite later uprisings, especially a major one in the 1780s, Spain continued to be in power until our independence was established in 1821.

Yes, there is a very factual, official history of Peru. But there is also a rich oral history of the Inca people that has been handed down for generations with many legends and a strong spiritual heritage. For me, these legends and traditions were to become as important as any fact ever written.

In the Inca spiritual tradition, all human beings are Children of the Sun. Every day we enjoy the light and warmth of the physical Father Sun. Behind our Father Sun we also have the "Sun behind the sun," or the Divine Presence, Who sends the life force energy through the Father Sun to Mother Earth for all people and all of nature. We receive this spiritual light energy in our spiritual body, from which it then flows to our physical body. In the spiritual body we can find the essence of the authentic self, for each of us is a unique ray from the same Sun. When we do not connect with this part of ourselves, we feel emptiness.

For many years, I tried to distance myself from this spiritual heritage to be a modern scientific man. Fortunately for me, the Cosmos kept presenting me with unusual experiences that reshaped my thoughts. Through many strange events and the guidance of many wonderful people, I found that I could immerse myself in my spiritual heritage and still hold on to today's world with its science and fantastic technology. At first I was reluctant to accept that I needed to be in touch with my spirit. I did not want to be a part of what I thought was superstition. But a seed of truth was growing inside of me. Little by little, I began to experience a knowing from my heart, beyond my mind. I found myself paying attention to my inner urges and feelings, my knowing and experiences, which were not coming from my intellect. Over time, so many things happened that I could no longer deny I was more than my mind, more than my body, more than my senses.

And a funny thing happened: the more I listened to my spirit, my heart, the more I succeeded in everyday life and my business. It all was connected. This also fits the Inca tradition that the purpose of life is to celebrate life, all of life. In my awakening, I found that my Inca heritage was based on living with a cosmic awareness. In this expanded reality, all of the scientific knowledge of the day is real, while we also experience our spiritual knowing and many other realities. Since I have awakened to an expanded existence, I have embraced my spiritual heritage, and my life is richer and more enjoyable. My heritage is beautiful and ever more meaningful to me.

Many people in the world fear that there will be major change with many catastrophes in the coming years. In the Inca world, we do see change, perhaps difficult, but for us this is a change to a more spiritual and harmonious time. A legend lives in the Andean culture called Pachakuti. In the Inca language, it means the Return to the Essence of the Cosmos. We believe that there is a cosmic cycle of one thousand years, like the cycle of the daytime and nighttime. Five hundred years is daytime. Five hundred years is nighttime. When the Conquerors arrived, they arrived with the Sunset between 1492 and 1532. Now we are living in a "New Sunrise." And for us the sunrise is very special, because we believe that the "first light" is the food for the heart. Like all the sunrises everywhere in the world, it brings life-force energy. It is the moment when we awake. It is the moment when we remember the essence of who we are, the essence of the creation. This is a wonderful time to be alive.

With the New Sunrise comes the opportunity for all the Children of the Sun, all humanity, to comprehend from the heart the higher levels of consciousness. In the Andean World, we understand that we are never alone. We understand that everything is alive, a living being. We understand the Solar memory and the perfection of the Creation. We understand that, regardless of where we live or what our beliefs, we are all Incas, all Children of the Sun. It is time to awaken and remember the true Inca Laws of Love, Service, and Wisdom, so that these beliefs and traditions awaken the spirit within us. These Cosmic Laws are beyond time. They are more important today than ever before as the new technology brings us closer together in a world community.

In this current cycle of the Sunrise, the Sacred Sites and Energy Vortexes of the world are reactivating, especially the Sacred Sites of Peru. All the special places are speaking – are healing – are opening doorways for the pilgrims. These Sacred Sites want us to follow the dream of the Apus, Mountain Light Beings, the dream of returning to our true spiritual heritage. On the cover of this book is a beautiful portal, a doorway. This is Aramu Muru's Doorway that can transport you to a different dimension. In many ways, each place or sacred site is a portal where you have the opportunity to connect to your spirit within. Each experience and each place in the book helped me to connect to my own spiritual body, my authentic self.

Every person is unique and awakens to the inner Divine in a slightly different way. I say "awakens" because your spiritual body is always with you, a natural and essential part of you. It is different than your mind and can only be experienced, not studied or understood by the mind. By awakening to your own spiritual being, you can enter into a fuller experience of this life. You can enter into your creative fountain of ideas and energy that comes from your own spirit and is never-ending. You can truly live a more satisfying and complete life each day.

Now, in the New Sunrise, is the time for all of people to become fully aware and see all things in the light of the New Day. We are being called to an expanded and unique way of living as individual rays of the one Father Sun. So, all people, from all traditions, can increase their enjoyment and experience of life every day. As we start to fully experience and know the authentic spiritual self, a new dream and a new spiral of abundance and prosperity also awakens. The Sunrise brings the new state of consciousness. This spiritual activation is taking place within each person's own belief system and in traditions all over the world. Perhaps a journey into the beliefs of the Andes will help connect you to a richer experience of your daily life and to the Divine within.

I offer you my services as an Inca guide to mystical Peru and to the awakening of your authentic self. Come travel with me.

# ARAMU MURU'S DOORWAY

# The Dream

Over and over, I kept having the same dream.

According to Andean legend, when the Spanish arrived in South America, a golden disc that held the record of many ancient civilizations was taken from the capital city of Cusco to the Monastery of the Seven Rays, and later hidden in a crystal city in the depths of Lake Titicaca. In my recurring dream, I was saying goodbye to my friends and walking in the direction of the Monastery of the Seven Rays. I was walking past some pink stones, like sandstones. Always, just as I was about to arrive at my destination, I awoke, startled and uneasy.

As this dream came again and again, it became increasingly important to me to know the meaning and why I never got to the monastery. Finally, I decided to ask for help from one of my friends, an Andean "priest." The Inca heritage comes from ancient times and is a way of interacting and thinking about all of creation rather than a particular religion. We call Andean priests *yatiri* in the Aymara language, which is the language of my heritage. I grew up speaking Aymara at home, Quechua in the marketplace, and Spanish at school.

My friend, Don Alejandro, whom I respected for his wisdom and down-to-earth attitude was an Aymara yatiris living in Puno, a city on the northern shore of Lake Titicaca. I called Don Alejandro and asked him to spend a day with me high in the altiplano near Puno. There are many special sacred sites in the altiplano that I thought could be a good place to work on the dream with Don Alejandro. The altiplano is rugged, beautiful, and vast. Don Alejandro did not think that we needed to go very far. He chose *Ichu*, a region of the high plateau, about a twenty-minute drive southwest of Puno.

# Inca Tunuhwire

Ichu is a little valley with fertile land that is known for growing onions. The people here came from Ecuador in pre-Incan times. At first, I wondered why Don Alejandro chose this place. Then, during the drive to Ichu, I remembered that there were many interesting formations in the sandstones throughout this valley. One of the formations was referred to as "the wedding," while others were recognized as "temples," or identified by their animal silhouettes. It is very similar to Sedona in Arizona. Ah, I thought, perhaps this is the place of my dreams. There are many, many legends about this valley. There are pre-Incan temples located here, as well as numerous stone formations. One very old legend says that the tops of the mountains are really "sleeping giants," another form of humanity that lived in this place many, many eons ago. Seeing the "faces" of these mountaintops can make you a believer.

When we arrived, the day was sunny, like most of the days of the year on the high plateau. We immediately hiked a bit up a hill to Inca Tunuhwire, a pre-Incan temple with a monolith that we call "Solar Plexus." This large stone is carved in human form with a hole at the place of the solar plexus. It has its arms bent and the palms of its hands are open, facing the Father Sun. Don Alejandro and I went and sat on a small rise that sat above the ancient temple. The sun reached down and touched the lake, which transformed into sapphire blue crystals dancing in the breeze. Illampu, an Apu or Mountain Spirit of the Royal Cordillera Mountain Range watched us from atop the looming snowcapped mountain across the lake.

Don Alejandro sat for a while after he heard my dream. He looked directly into my eyes. Don Alejandro was a rather tall man with a tanned square face. His intense black eyes seemed to pierce directly into my soul. I knew that he thought the dream was very important. He finally said, "Any dream that repeats many times is in this level of reality, as well as other levels. Finding the place in this reality will bring important answers in your own spiritual quest. Then you will remember and then you will know." He told me to try to find the actual place that I saw in my dreams. "The Monastery?" I asked. "No," he replied, "First you have to find the pink sandstone place, which exists in this reality, not only in your dreams. There must be something special for you there."

A short time after that day I spent with Don Alejandro, I returned to Ichu and searched the entire area. I experienced many strong feelings there. I walked in all directions searching for something that matched the dream. I found that the sandstone had been used as ancient shrines. There were many natural and several artfully carved designs and images. Yet nothing resonated with the dream. I left somewhat discouraged. Then it occurred to me that this place was similar to Copamaya, Tiawanaku, and Pucara. All three places were pre-Incan shrines chosen by the people, in part, for their mystical sandstone formations. Maybe my answer would be in one of these spiritual sites that also had stone statues or monoliths and majestic walls of massive stones. Since Copamaya was closest, I decided to go there first.

# Copamaya

There are many legends and much mystery surrounding the word "Copa" from pre-Inca times. This word begins the name of many special places like Copamaya, Copacati, and Copacabana. All three of these sacred sites are on the shores of Lake Titicaca facing the vital center of the Lake. In fact, one of the age-old names of Lake Titicaca is Winay Marka, the Eternal City. In the ancient traditions, the Eternal City is where the Light Beings of the Spirit realm lived. So it seemed reasonable to me that Copamaya could be the place I visited in my dream.

I arrived late in the morning. You have to climb up through a small rural community to access the shrine, located on a ledge overlooking this community and Lake Titicaca. On my way up the path, a teenage girl greeted me. I told her I wanted to go up to the shrine. She accompanied me to her nearby home, which was tucked into an area that was bordered by hedges and stone formations. I greeted the girl's father, Pedro, and again explained that I was hiking up to the Copamaya shrine. Pedro was very welcoming and allowed me to walk through his property. I asked him why he had chosen to build his house here on the side of the hill so high. Pedro explained, "We have to obey Pachamama. We talk to Her through the coca leaves. By reading the coca leaves, we know where the Mother wants us to live, where the animals are to live, and where the plants are to live." *Pachamama* is our name for Mother Earth as *Inti* is for Father Sun. In our tradition, Pachamama and Inti are alive conscious beings. They are the very expressions of the Divine Creator that support our very existence.

His daughter, my guide, Rita, picked fuchsia-like red flowers, called *kantuta*, for me to take as an offering to the shrine. I accepted the flowers and thanked her. The kantuta is also called the Inca flower, and it is a sign of hospitality. It is traditionally used in all of the Andes for welcoming people to your home. As I was leaving, Pedro invited me to join his family for their noon meal after my visit to the shrine.

With these flowers and this *chuyma* (a welcome from the heart), I arrived at the monolithic cliff. From one piece of sandstone there are three levels of carved shrines. All three shrines are facing the "Eternal City" and the Sacred Islands within the "Lake Womb of the Mother," Lake Titicaca. I climbed up and over the narrow ledges to one indentation on the second level of the shrine. I stood with my back to the monolithic wall and opened my arms, my mind, and my heart to the Lake. The Lake was blue, turquoise, and green, blending all at the same time. Since it was still morning, the Lake had some of the intense blue color that kisses it every morning with the dawn. It was a magnificent feeling of beauty, freedom and promise. Copamaya had many of the aspects and feelings of my dream, but it was not the exact place of the dream. I continued my search.

# Three Teenagers

The noon meal, or lunch, is the main meal in the Andean Highlands. It was very gracious of Pedro and his family to invite me to join them. The preparation of the meal would have started very early in the morning. During the time of the harvest, people in the highlands have a very special way of preparing the newly harvested potatoes. The potatoes are dug from the mud with a sickle-like tool called a *raocana*. Some of the clay comes up in clumps, encasing the potatoes. The people take this clay and pile it up like bricks to form an outdoor oven. They put some wood and dried herbs in the oven and light it. As the oven becomes very hot, the ashes are removed from the side of the oven, and a hole is carved out of the top by removing some of the clay. The clay is then crumbled into the oven, and the potatoes are added. The potatoes bake in the oven for a couple of hours. Then they are served on a piece of hand-woven fabric along with wheat soup and pieces of lamb. The crumbled clay, *chaco*, is mixed with water and salt to make a form of salsa, and is also used as a medication. The food was simple, but delicious. I was content as I enjoyed the hospitality of this lively family.

As I was eating, I remembered the legend that talks about the origin of the potato. The legend came from Iscata, the Region of Copamaya. I asked Rita if she knew of this legend. She said yes, but her little sisters (ages five and six) did not know it. I decided to introduce the little girls to the legend.

I began, "A long time ago, three teenage girls were walking around the lake. At sunset it started to get cold and dark. They realized that they could not return to their home before dark, so they walked to the nearest house that they could find. This house belonged to an Aymara family. The family was curious about the three girls and where they came from. They were definitely not members of the local community.

"The family instantly welcomed the girls, making them feel very special. The three girls were invited to stay the night with the family. The family gave them reed mattresses, alpaca wool covers, and some other warm blankets. They all enjoyed an evening meal of herbal soup and tea. After they talked a bit about their journey, the girls retired to their room. They never said exactly where they had come from or where they were going.

The next day, at sunrise, the owner of the house went to invite the girls for breakfast. When he knocked on the door of their room, no one answered. After a few moments of knocking and waiting, he decided to open the door to see why they did not answer. The man was deeply surprised when the room was empty. He thought that this was very strange. He always awakened very early and had not heard anyone leave. Also, the dogs had not barked. They surely would have roused if the girls had left the house. With a surprised expression on his face, he said to himself, "This is very strange." He was about to close the door when he noticed something. Nestled in one corner of the room were what looked like three tubers. He was curious about them and went over to examine the strange tubers. They seemed to be a form of plant like a yucca, but he had not seen anything quite like them before. He thought that maybe the girls had accidentally forgotten them. He hoped that the girls would return for them.

"After waiting almost three months, the man decided to plant the tubers. The girls had not returned, and the tubers were starting to get very dry. It was the planting season, so he planted them in a field near the house. When the plants started to grow and their first flowers bloomed, the Aymara man noticed something oddly familiar about these plants. The leaves and flowers vaguely reminded him of someone. One day he decided to talk to the plants, as Aymara people often do. Suddenly, he recognized the plants. They actually were the teenage girls that had visited his family. The plants told him that they were a gift from the Mother Earth to the family for their hospitality and care of the teenage girls.

"Since that very day, potatoes are considered to be girls. Many names for the potato start with *imilla* (girl in Spanish), like imilla blanca, or imilla negra. That is why every time we plant or harvest the potato, we have a special ceremony giving gratitude to Mother Earth for her gift. This is why today, during the fiestas, the teenagers are the ones who traditionally play the games with the potatoes. The teenage boys throw the potato flower buds at the teenage girls, who, of course, like the attention very much. They are still honoring the original teenage imillas."

# Bebedero del Inca

Some weeks after I had spent the day at Copamaya, I thought of another place with sandstones. I used to visit this place in my work as a tour guide. It is called Bebedero del Inca, the drinking place of the Incas. The Spanish thought that this was the place where the people drink *chicha*. (homemade corn beer). The fact is that Bebedero del Inca is an ancient place for ceremonies. The ceremony utilizes chicha, as well as coca leaves, because the ceremony requires the presence of *Mama Sara* (Mother Corn) and *Mama Coca* (Mother Coca). The title, Mother, indicates that the people recognize that these plants care for and nurture them.

Bebedero del Inca is close to Lake Titicaca, but is not located on the shores of the lake. This ancient site sits inland, about two kilometers from the lake, and very close to the Pan-American highway. As soon as I had some free time, I decided to go walking at Bebdero Del Inca. Because of the many sandstones and special formations in the surrounding area, I had been experiencing the dream even more frequently. At least four times, I awoke just as I was arriving at a special place in the dream. My frustration and curiosity were growing, and I thought about the dream every day.

When I actually did arrive at Bebedero del Inca, I saw the place with different eyes than I had as a tour guide. I had prepared myself to approach this familiar place in a much more ceremonial way. As soon as I arrived, I spent time connecting to my own energy, my own spiritual self. Since I routinely practiced connecting to my energy, it took me only a few moments to silence and empty my mind and become aware of all my senses. There are many more than five senses, and I focused all of my senses to be in tune with all the realities of the ancient site.

I was immediately aware of many things that had not been apparent to me on previous visits. Bebedero del Inca is another pre-Incan site that has large monolithic stonewalls and sandstone formations. I became intensely aware of the many shrines and altars within this natural landscape temple. A sense of familiarity came over me. I was ready to explore this wonderful monument in hopes of finding the exact place I was seeking in the dream.

# Reading the Stones

The warming sun had risen over the lake only an hour before I arrived at Bebedero del Inca. This is the perfect time to come here. Father Sun is low in the sky and casts shadows on the rocks. The entire area was bathed in the early light. The area was engulfed in the mystical cloak of light, even though the highway was only a few steps away. The sandstones seemed even pinker in color than usual, and the rock clusters on the flat landscape felt alive and robust. I was enjoying the forms and their shadows as I approached the first grouping of rocks. I felt like a mystical explorer as I climbed the nearby sandstone cluster. The increasing sunlight illuminated every aspect of the texture of the stone's surface.

On top of a half-circle natural rock shrine in the first stone cluster, I noticed four distinct indentations. I began to see the shape of the Puma paw carved into the stone. Anchored in the stone was an etheric Puma. To make the presence of the etheric Puma evident, our ancestors carved these four puma footprints. Using coca leaves and chicha symbols of spiritual and physical food, I asked permission from the etheric Puma to explore this area. I formed the coca leaves into a *kintui* (three coca leaves placed on top of each other in a fan like fashion) and placed them in the Puma's footprints. I anchored the offering with the chicha, by pouring it into the indentation of the Puma footprint. I then noticed two larger imprints, the size of the human foot, carved into a large rock next to the stone cluster containing the paw prints. I decided to "stand there," lying down on the side of the sloping rock with my feet in the larger holes to keep myself secure.

Through an inner voice, the rock invited me to open my arms. When I opened my arms, I noticed I was facing east, looking across the Lake at Sun Island and Illampu. This rock was surprisingly comfortable. It gently supported my spinal column and embraced my whole body. When I opened my arms, my body had such a natural affinity with the rock that I was totally content lying there. There was even more joy when I closed my physical eyes and could feel in my heart the connection to the light of the Father Sun. I realized that this was a place to receive the First Light of daybreak that opens your heart spiritually. It seemed that my heart expanded with the opening of my arms. A sense of joy and calm overtook me, and I thought, "The Spanish were right! This is the place to drink, but to drink Light."

After this fulfilling experience, I felt energized. I was mysteriously drawn to walk on the right side of the landscape shrine. I climbed nine steps to reach the top of the extended rock formation. I looked across the mound of rocks extending about one hundred yards in length and varying from four to ten yards high in an undulating fashion. I started to walk along the top. It was precariously narrow in places, but I enjoyed the sensation. As I was walking, I wanted to be "one" with the stones. I felt the child in me playing "follow the leader." The stones were very enticing.

The thought entered my consciousness that I was walking on top of the back of the ethereal Snake, connecting me to the Lower or Underground World. I did not feel any heaviness. Instead, I still had a very special feeling – like a kid playing, enjoying balancing on the stones. I opened my arms as if I were flying across the stones. As I reached the end of the Snake, I saw the form of the back of the Puma with its tail so perfectly connected to the Snake. The child in me ran down the tail to the ground. With the Snake and the Puma (representing this Middle World), I expected the Condor (representing the Upper World) to be close by. I noticed that the Snake and the Puma were aligned in a common direction with one another. I sensed that they were interconnected by the Earth's magnetic energy grid. I decided to follow this energy or *ley line* until I got to the top of a small hill, and I was able to observe the natural formation of the stones from above. There in front of me, manifested in the rock, was the presence and appearance of an old Condor. I immediately realized that this was a place where we could connect with the Cosmos through the Inca cosmic messenger, the Condor. In this natural landscape shrine, I realized that I could connect to all three worlds within the Inca tradition.

# City of Spirits

I stood there scanning the panoramic view of this valley with large sandstone formations. I gradually started to physically see many forms visible in the rock clusters. In some places, there were tall, solid walls and columns. In other places, there appeared a face, or the form of an ancient animal. There was a "family" of faces going up the side of one high rock formation, with five faces of different ages and sizes. Looking at all of this, I remembered the ancient name of this place – Ajayu Marca (City of the Spirits).

The local people have many ancient legends surrounding this valley.

One of the legends is about the musicians who disappeared here, never to be seen again. There are also legends concerning the faces and animals. There is the "tired horse" legend of the Inca with his horse that was carrying gold. Exhausted from their endeavor, they got tired and stopped here to rest, and turned into stone. Other stories accompany the horse, the rabbit, the guinea pig, the elephant, and the dinosaurs. The stone butterflies look down from their perch high on the side of a cliff at a twenty-foot-long stone caterpillar that has been ever so slowly crossing the valley for untold eons.

I reverently walked through this valley for about an hour, looking at the rocks. I was very curious, and yet, I had no real expectations. I was now walking in the dream. I had found the exact place manifested from my dream.

# The Discovery

Following the ley line, I was led down into the valley to my left. I soon became aware of a large natural pink sandstone wall on my right. It was approximately eighteen feet wide and twenty-one feet high. It appeared to be very ancient. A mysterious stone portal caught my attention. As I got closer, I sensed that the portal, or doorway, was of another dimension. Immediately, I was filled with a sense of reverence. I asked permission of the Spirit Guardian of the place to approach the doorway. It is an Andean tradition that there is a Spirit Guardian of all locations, especially Sacred Places. As is our custom, I asked permission of the Guardian before entering their domain. I knelt in front of the doorway with my hands resting on the steps situated on either side of the doorway. I then put my head on the rock and noticed that there was a little hole there, exactly at the point of my third eye (an opening to the intuitive mind that sits triangularly on the forehead between the two eyes). After a few moments of inner calm, I stood up and entered the twelve-inch indentation of the doorway. I stretched out my arms with the palms of my hands on each side of the doorway. It seemed as if the doorway was made to fit exactly a person my size. It felt like I had penetrated deep inside myself and deep inside the natural rock structure simultaneously.

The next thing in my awareness was the sensation of floating colors and accompanying chills. Following this, I had an intense feeling of warmth and visualized an iridescent white cloth engulfing my body. I experienced many visions while standing in the doorway. I do not know how long I stood there in this state of bliss and humility. Gently, the doorway released me and I stepped back, filled with gratitude. As I stood there looking at the doorway, two columns became apparent to me. Each column was twenty feet tall, hollow, and standing on different sides of the doorway. I stood in each column and experienced energy spinning in opposite directions, a characteristic of an energy vortex. This entire experience left me feeling calm, yet energized.

As I stepped back and peered at the doorway, I reflected on the most meaningful vision I had while I was standing in the doorway. In the vision, I saw the back of a man walking through the doorway and disappearing into the wall. The inner knowing of my open heart then made it apparent to my conscious mind that the man was Master *Aramu Muru* as he passed through this doorway into another dimension.

One of the legends of Aramu Muru is associated with the Golden Disc of the Incas. In the legend, Aramu Muru, brought a golden disc from *Lemuria* (legendary continent in ancient times) as a symbol of humanity's connection to *Hatun Inti* (Divine Central Sun). Lemuria, an advanced civilization on a massive continent in the Pacific Ocean, sank before the Andes Mountains were born. When Aramu Muru decided to leave this reality, it is said that he went to Lake Titicaca and walked through a doorway to an unknown mystical dimension.

# Arrival of PachaKuti

The impact of my experience at the mystical portal led me to share this newfound information with a few friends in the travel agencies. Initially, Don Alejandro read the coca leaves and said that it was not the correct time to take many people to the doorway. I followed the advice of his reading and only took a few very close friends to the site. Several years later, Don Alejandro acknowledged that the time had come to invite other people to experience the doorway. In 1992, I started the practice of taking travelers to the doorway. Coincidently, in the Inca tradition, 1992 marks the beginning of the transition into *PachaKuti*, the beginning of the new five-hundred-years-cycle of the Cosmos. The Children of the Sun believe that we are now in the beginning of the New Sunrise of five hundred years of the daytime (light) after five hundred years of the night (darkness). We believe that the Spanish arrived in the Americas at the Sunset of the last light-cycle. During the year 1992, there were many ceremonies held around the world on November 11 (11-11-92) to increase the expansion of consciousness. "Eco 92" was held in Brazil among world leaders to address the care of Mother Earth. Many people, of many traditions, seemed to sense a change in consciousness and a shift in the Cosmos. The Incas sensed a New Sunrise.

The promise of PachaKuti and the New Sunrise is the return of the time for the Children of the Sun. It is the time to recognize the concepts defining the Children of the Sun in all of us. It is a time of awakening and remembering who we really are, with a new vision of this reality. It is time for a change of paradigm. It is a time of opportunity for great expansions of consciousness. It is the time for all humanity, as Children of the Sun, to open their hearts and live in joy and abundance. It is the time for the Children of the Sun to live in balance, harmony, and *ayni*, reciprocity with all of nature. It is the time of the new cycle. It is the time of PachaKuti

When I first invited people to the doorway, I knew of no name for it. I was curious and asked many local people about existing names. I found that an ancient traditional name for the portal was Wilka Uta, meaning the House of Divinity, the House of the Sun. Another name was Altarani, meaning the place with the altar. The name that the Spanish used, to deter the people from visiting this place, was the Devil's Doorway. Later, I talked with a journalist from Europe who interviewed me about the doorway's history. He published the interview with the title, "The re-discovery of the Mysterious Aramu Muru doorway." I didn't say that this was the Aramu Muru doorway. What I explained to him was that my personal experience was with Aramu Muru. After this article was published, I noticed that in other magazines and books, it was called Aramu Muru Doorway. Now, even the local people have adopted this name for the doorway.

# Path of the Chacaruna

As I reflect on the moments when I first stood in the Aramu Muru Doorway, I realize that this experience was an expanding "bridge" for me into other dimensions and other realities. And I was becoming, more and more, a "bridge person," a *chacaruna* in the Quechua language. A chacaruna is the one who helps others to cross from "one side of the river to the other side," from one state of consciousness to other states of consciousness. He can also form a bridge from the mind to the heart and from the present to the past or to the future. A chacaruna is always exploring this reality to connect with the beauty and perfection of the Creation. Chacarunas travel their path quietly. They do not call attention to themselves in the community, but they offer their service in a variety of ways. They offer special ceremonies and teachings that can help the people connect to the Spirit world and to their own spiritual being. At the deepest level, a chacaruna is the one who can "walk" between several worlds, including the upper world, this or middle world, and the lower world.

Many of the people on this path call themselves shamans. The word shaman is not native to the Andes. In fact, I do not want to be a shaman in the sense that I have special, magical powers. Everybody has the power to connect to the Divine. I do accept that I have been given gifts that can help others discover their authentic spiritual being. When you choose the pathway of Spirit, the Cosmos gradually unfolds certain gifts, which activate the chacaruna's abilities to work with many different manifestations of the Cosmos. It doesn't happen in a moment or at any particular time. He grows in awareness and begins to recognize his particular "gifts" when his services are accepted and recognized by the people. I did not set out on a spiritual path, not even after I mysteriously received a special crystal. I became more aware that I was on the path of the chacaruna in the special moments of discovering, actually re-discovering, the "Doorway."

One marvelous thing about being a chacaruna is that your path and spiritual expression is unique. The experience of the Doorway was to greatly influence the shaping of my path. Don Alejandra was correct in saying that it was important for me to find the location of my dream in the present reality first. What I experienced in my mind and heart in re-discovering the Aramu Muru Doorway was and still is very special for me.

It had not been my intention or desire to be on this path. However, no matter how I tried to avoid the study and knowledge of the Cosmos, I was drawn back to the path in some way. My mother, who is an Aymara healer, has quietly watched my unique quest with a loving and knowing heart. She never tried to direct me to the path, but has been there to witness, as I first avoided, and then embraced my spiritual quest.

# AYMARA HERITAGE

My mother, Margarita, is from a small community of Aymara people in the Highland near Lake Titicaca. She is a quiet, active person, who moved from her original community at a very young age to work in other villages in the highlands (over 14,000 feet in altitude). Although the people of this region did not record age, my mother was married at a traditional young age to a schoolteacher, Carlos Delgado. My father came from the other side of the Lake near the border with Bolivia. My mother rarely speaks of the time she started to do healings with children. After my mother and father married, they had their first child. My mother's grandmother, Paula Paquita, began to teach her how to heal children. My mother's father, Don Justo, and her brother, Mariano, were both respected yatiris. My grandfather and uncle were both known for their special ceremonies with incense for blessing houses and cleansing them of their heavy (negative) energies. My mother mainly worked with the children of family and friends. Although she did not want to be well known as a healer, many neighbors and their friends sought her help with their children.

My grandfather, Don Justo, also raised llamas and alpacas in the highlands. I was about ten years old when, for the first time, I went to visit him and spent time at his home without my parents. It was very cold in the high altitude of the upper highlands, and only *ichu* grass would grow in these conditions. This long grass was enough food to nourish the llamas and alpacas. Since not much else would grow here, this land was only used to herd animals. One of my clearest memories is of the day that my grandfather sent me out to lead the alpacas back from their grazing in the late afternoon. I felt very important having this responsibility. A couple of days later, I realized that the alpacas knew when and how to return on their own. Perhaps they were taking care of me! I was fascinated to observe that when the animals did return from the fields, they went back to the exact same space to sleep. They always slept in exactly the same position, in exactly the same location.

While I have fond memories of my grandfather, I was then more interested in his animals than in his ceremonies. I never thought of him as a respected yatiri. I did know my uncle Mariano as a yatiri. My uncle would often come to Puno, the city on Lake Titicaca where I lived. He and my mother would conduct the ceremonies for cleansing the houses in and around Puno.

When I was young, I had little interest in their ceremonies or any aspect of spirituality. I knew that my mother did healings, but I never witnessed her performing them. My mother was also very busy raising ten children.

Every Sunday I accompanied her to the local outdoor markets in the communities to sell products like corn, fruits, and other produce. We would first purchase these products in Puno, and then take them to the highlands to sell for a little profit. In return, my mother would then buy meat and other necessities that people brought from their villages to the marketplace. I would help her carry, as well as sell, the products. I loved going to the marketplace because it was so crowded and alive. All of the people were colorfully dressed in the patterns and fabrics of their local communities. You can recognize the men from each community by the distinctive pattern of their knitted hats.

We would usually see many of our relatives in the marketplace and catch up on all the family news. Before departing, we collected sand from the river and put it in bags to carry back to our community. Since we were building a house, we took advantage of the opportunity to return home with the sand after selling our goods. We never returned to Puno empty handed. My family was slowly building a house, room by room, as was the custom. We could build only as we were able to buy or collect the materials. The entire family lived in one room for years before we could expand by adding a second room. Although the conditions were crowded, we were happy and found this to be manageable.

# Cholla

My mother always wore skirts with petticoats and a *manta* (native shawl). On her head she wore a bowler hat. The bowler hat originated from English influence. English engineers came to Peru to build the railway in 1875. The English always wore bowler hats. The Andean ladies liked these hats very much. Since that time, the women in the High Plateau of the Andes have worn bowler hats every day as part of their native garb. There was a rebellion of the indigenous people against the colonial government in 1779–80. The indigenous leaders were Tupa Amaru of the Quechua people and Tupac Katari of the Aymara people. Even today, most of the indigenous people still speak either Quechua or Aymara. The rebellion was unsuccessful. Afterward, the Spanish government banned the people of the highlands from wearing their former native clothing. Wearing native clothing was considered to be a symbol of the rebellion against the government. Thereafter, the people wore clothing with a European influence called *cholla* for the ladies and *chollo* for the men. Today, you can still see a definite European influence in the everyday native clothing of the indigenous people of the Andean High Plateau (under 14000 feet in altitude) and the highlands.

# Healing the Babies

People came to my house and took my mother to their house expecting that she would bring comfort and spiritual harmony to their ill babies. The babies could not tell anyone what was bothering them. My mother would collect some of the baby's clothes, carrying them as she walked for hours in the mountains. Calling aloud the name of the baby, my mother would converse with the Spirit of the mountain and then return to the baby's house at sunset. If she could not go to the mountains, my mother would walk around the house praying for the child. She would then call the Apu from the doorway of the house. She would cover the baby with the clothes or blanket and reconcile the baby's soul with the baby's physical body. Often, she would gently massage the baby's body. Occasionally, people would come from as far away as twenty miles to have my mother heal their baby's distress. They sought my mother's help and greatly respected her gifts. I tended to take her ministrations for granted. I paid little attention to my mother's healings unless they involved me.

Many highland people believe when a child falls and is injured, the child needs to eat a little bit of the dirt from the place where they were injured. This helps them conquer their fear of this place and prevent scarring. They believe that physical scarring comes from an internal fear that manifests as an outward sign of the fear. If a child developed a scar, the parents would bring the child to my mother for her to heal the child's internal fear so that the scar would go away. I remember one time that I fell and my mother had me eat a pinch of the dirt. I don't know if I had internal fear or not, but I never got a scar.

# Puno

Nestled on the side of a small mountain in an upper corner of Lake Titicaca is the City of Puno. According to the legends, the first Inca rose from the Lake and traveled by what is now Puno on his way to Cusco. Later, the Inca returned to the Lake and stopped to rest in Puno, which comes from *puñuy*, meaning "place to sleep."

I was about three or four years old when my family moved to this city, and I vividly recall memories of kindergarten. I always loved school and as I grew older I came to appreciate that in the city I was able to attend school, while in the villages, education was more limited. Today, Puno is still my home and has retained some remnants of the civilization that lived here in pre-Incan times. Today, as capital of the Region, Puno city is a center for culture, folklore, and the arts. The most important offices of the government are located in Puno. The Spaniards expanded the city in colonial times because of the nearby silver mines. Since Puno sits on Lake Titicaca, it is also an important mercantile port. From years ago, I can remember hearing the sound of the large steam ships leaving the port, heading to Bolivia.

Each year in February, my city has its major festival and it is possibly the largest festival in Peru. The two-week festival is to honor the Madonna of Candelaria. Dancers gather from all the different neighborhoods. During the festival you can observe over three hundred different folk dances. Hundreds of people will join in the festivities by dancing in the streets. The competing dancers, all in costume, enact small vignettes with their dancing. One group of dancers can have three to five hundred members dancing. Thousands of people attend to both celebrate and keep their folk traditions vibrant and alive.

*Juliaca*, which is now a slightly larger neighboring city to the north of Puno, is flat in topography and a growing commercial center. Both cities have areas that are quite modern mixed with other areas that are more village-like. Reflecting the different cultures within the cities, there are many cars, vans, and trucks sharing the roadway with our "ecological taxis," tricycles that can transport two people or products through the streets. While there are many tricycles in Puno, I think that maybe there are more tricycles than people in Juliaca!

# Mysterious Lady

As a child growing up, I enjoyed the folklore of my city, but I paid little attention to the ceremonial heritage of my family. I was not very interested in what my mother did with the babies. By the age of ten or eleven years, I was more interested in going to school and making some money to help at home. When I was eleven years old, there was an incident that was to be very important to me later in my life. I used to take people from the bus station and train station to the hotels, helping with their suitcases and packages. Because of the times and our needs, I had to make some money to help support our large family.

One day, a lady arrived from Arequipa, a large city in a neighboring region of Peru, between the Andes and the coast. The lady arrived at the train station in the afternoon and asked me to take her to her hotel. There were only two blocks to the hotel, so I was happy to have this job. I said, "We can do that." She asked me to wait for her while she checked into the hotel and asked me to take her to a restaurant. I waited as she requested, and took her to a very nice restaurant. When we arrived at the restaurant she wanted me to go into the restaurant with her and have something to eat. I did not want to go in, but she pulled me in. That was the first time I was ever in a restaurant. I was unsure of myself and a little bit shy. Actually, I was afraid of the place. So, I said to her, "You know, I'd better go." She said, "No, no, stay!"

We sat down and the lady started to cry. I thought to myself, "Something is going on here. I'd better go." I was trying to move, to escape in some way. But she took my hand and said, "Don't worry, I am talking with God." Then I was really worried. I said, "Oh, this is crazy. I need to go home." She said, "Okay, we are going to your home." I said, "No, no way, impossible!"

The waiter brought the food and we ate. I was trying to explain to her, "It's difficult to get to my house. It's far away. The taxis don't go there. There is a river in between and only tiny boats." I was trying to convince her that her escorting me home was a bad idea. I thought my family would be very upset to have this lady, this stranger, come to the house. My parents had just one room finished in the house, and the other room was in the process of being built. Building was very slow because the banks did not offer credit. In those days, we had to build only with the cash a family could save.

So I said, "No, no, no!" But she kept asking me until I finally agreed, and we started to walk. It was possible to take a taxi, but I thought that if we walked she would get tired and stop. The lady never even slowed down. To my surprise and dismay, she even took off her shoes and crossed the narrow, shallow river.

# Unexpected Ceremony

When the lady and I arrived at my home, I was very worried about my predicament. What were my parents going to say to me about bringing somebody home that nobody knows? I thought, "Okay, we'll see what happens." When we arrived at my home, the dog was barking. While I went to tie up the dog, the lady just walked straight into the house. She was starting a ceremony when I rushed inside. I was surprised that she had just walked in, but my biggest surprise was that nobody in my family was complaining. I didn't understand it. Even my brothers and sisters were joining in the ceremony. Somebody said, "Put something white on your head." The lady just walked in and performed a ceremony. It was interesting because, when she finished the ceremony, she gave some money to my mother. It was a lot of money at that time, and we needed the money. But my mother never spent that money until much later, after it lost almost all its value because of inflation and Peru changed the currency. Instead of spending the lady's gift, my mother used it as a talisman, an amulet. My mother kept the money in a knitted bag, shaped like a wine bottle. The bag was very colorful and had a pocket for special red and black ceremonial beans, as well as a narrow opening at the top. Rather than use this considerable amount of money, my mother continued working to feed the family.

The day got even more interesting when the lady asked me to take her back to the train station and buy her a ticket for Arequipa for that same day. She arrived from Arequipa just a few hours before and now she was asking me to take her to the station to return to Arequipa. I thought, "What's going on here?" She didn't use the hotel. She didn't use any of the tours to the three islands on the Lake – the typical places that everybody arrives to see. Nothing! I asked her, "Why are you leaving?" "Because I finished my work," she said. I thought, what kind of work does she do? She arrived at the train station, went to my house and now she is here buying a ticket to return. There was no work. What is she doing, I wondered. But she just left. I found out later that she told my mother that I was "very special to God," and my mother cried. This was just too weird for me. I tried to forget about the lady as I went about my daily routine. Still, sometimes thoughts of her would sneak into my mind as I went to the train station to find work.

# Pre-Incan to Incan Heritage

Growing up in Puno and going to the marketplace with my mother, I learned Aymara and Quechua, as well as Spanish. My mother spoke three languages and expected me to do the same. Knowing three languages was helpful in my finding jobs from a very early age. Later, as a tour guide, I learned a few more languages, including English.

Judging by language, we can say that Aymara is pre-Incan. Quechua is the better-known language of the Incas. However, both languages were spoken during the time of the Incas in the Andes. Since every community in the Inca world was unique, customs and beliefs were similar, yet different, in all communities. Generally, the Aymara people have square faces. Their build is also quite square in dimension. The Quechua people have more elongated, oval faces and stand just a bit shorter and thinner than the Aymara.

Aymara textiles also differ from the Quechua handiwork. Both sides of the fabric will have a design in the Aymara textiles, while the Quechua only have designs woven into one side of the fabric. Both are on display at the Smithsonian Institute in Washington, D.C. The name, Aymara, comes from Haya Mara, meaning "from the old times." The language of the "old times" people is Haque Aru, which means "language of the people." Quechua is actually the name of a region in the Andeans between 8,400 feet to 10,500 feet above sea level. The real name of the language is Runa Simi, which also means "language of the people." The term "language of the people" indicates that there are other languages, such as languages of the plants, of the animals, etc. For the Andean people, there are more differences in language than in customs. Although the Aymara and Quechua often cannot speak each other's language, they do trade and barter in the marketplace without difficulty. These two groups make up the most significant population of the Andes. The Spanish conquerers divided Peru into three regions: costal, mountains, and jungle. Today, Peru has eight geographic regions.

# Interest Grows

While I was content with my heritage as an indigenous person, I lived with, but didn't pursue knowing anymore about, the Incas than was necessary in school. I even accepted the Inca Laws such as: don't be lazy, don't lie, and don't steal. There was no deep thought or interest on my part. I did very well in school, especially in history and mathematics, but the history was always related to me from the Spanish viewpoint. When I was young I didn't question what was taught about the Incas. I was more interested in playing or making a little money after school. It wasn't until I was a tour guide, taking groups of weavers to different areas of Peru to see the local textiles that my interest in the Inca world ignited. Textiles became a passion for me. I loved them all and soon had a collection of fabrics from every community. I was particularly drawn to the fabrics that had naturally dyed threads before the 1940's. In the Andes, people sell their textiles, new and old, in the marketplaces. They will also sell the ponchos and bags that they are wearing. I frequently acquired the most wonderful textiles right off peoples' backs! This passion started early in my career as a tour guide and continues to this day.

I started to collect antique *conopas*, *cuyas*, and *illas*. I found out that these pieces were important to the Inca people as ceremonial "power tools." Conopas are llamas, alpacas, and sometimes flowers carved from stone or crystal with one-inch-diameter holes bored on top in which to put llama fat or incense to burn. They were and continue to be placed in prominent locations in the homes as protectors of the home. Cuyas are healing stones, usually rounded, that are either placed directly on the person's body or in a piece of textile, which is then passed around the person's body or energy field. Rectangular, four- to five-inch alabaster stones carved in the form of animals, houses, and inhabitants are called *illas*. In essence, the illa is a *mesa* or altar unto itself. Although I didn't know about or have interest in the ceremonies, I loved these antiques. I started to buy and sell the pieces to make a little profit, but certain pieces I loved and kept for myself.

To be able to conduct different kinds of tours regarding the art and handicrafts of the people, I read all that I could find. I wasn't easily satisfied. I wanted to know more of the history of the antique power tools. The books often contained the opinions of outside experts about the antiquities and art of the Incas. The art of any people reveals their soul. Only the people creating the art can explain the true, inner meaning of their work. Little by little, I learned the traditions, customs, and beliefs of my people in the "traditional" Inca classroom by word of mouth in the communities. I learned my heritage in a meaningful and intoxicating manner. I would recommend this form of study to anyone who wants to know the factual information as well as the inner life of any people. Study the art and handicrafts of the people. In so doing, you will truly know, experience, and understand them.

# Madonna of the Lake

Lake Titicaca is an enormous body of water that is nestled in the Andes. One wonders at first glance, what such a large body of water is doing sitting so high among the majestic mountains of Peru and Bolivia. Many Madonnas are named for the lake in the neighboring communities. During the colonial times, communities around the lake were encouraged to choose a saint or a Madonna as a protector. This concept was very comfortable for the Inca people, who considered each location to have a Spirit called a Pachamama — sometimes referred to as little Pachamamas; Mother Earth is usually referred to as Pachamama.

On Lake Titicaca, the Madonna is honored with two different titles. One is Our Lady of Copacabana, a small town in Bolivia on the southern shore of the Lake. For some people, she is Amara Mara. For others she is Lady Eternity. She is the Madonna protector of Bolivia, and the Bolivians have yearly festivals in her honor, lasting for nearly two weeks. The second Madonna is Our Lady of Candelaria of Puno, Peru. It is the same Madonna. Each community has their own title. Both Bolivia and Peru, annually celebrate the feast of the Madonna on February second. In each festival there is a great deal of music, dancing, and celebration. The Lady of Candelaria is considered the Lady of the Three Fires (combustible, solar, and electrical). She is the Mother of the Mother of the Mother of the Fire. The Lady of Cadelaria is the Mother Igneos, the Mother of the Origin of the Fire.

Many people of the Andean tradition also think that "entities" of enchantment live in the lake. A friend told me of an experience he had while he was walking home along the lake after some revelry. He felt lucid and was walking directly to his house. He thought he was walking into his house when he heard the call of nearby boatmen who came to his aid. Half of his body was in the water when they stopped him and pulled him ashore. There are many strange stories about the enchantment of the lake.

# Sacred Lake

n the Andean tradition, Lake Titicaca is the Lake of the Origin of the People. Civilization started on the lake. It is considered the birthplace of the First Inca. The legend says *Manco Capac* and *Mama Ocllo* had been sent by the Father Sun to organize the people to help them live more harmoniously. The name Inca originally meant "the leader of the people." Later, all of the people came to be known as Incas. The Lake was the place on Mother Earth for the birth of the first Inca, who was sent to lead the people to the Father. Lake Titicaca is considered the Womb of Mother Earth. It is the seat of the feminine polarity of the planet. The masculine polarity is in Tibet, in the Himalaya Mountains. Interestingly, there is a word in Aymara, jinaalaya, which means "upstairs." I would not be surprised if there was intercommunication between the people living in the areas of the two polarities in ancient times. I do know that llamas from Tibet are now visiting the Lake in increasing numbers. The name of the region of the Sacred Lake in Quechua is Pakarina. *Mama Cocha* is the Quechua name for the Spirit of all lakes and seas. Mama Cocha is the Mother of the Lake. In the Inca tradition, this identification lasts to this day, all bodies of water are feminine. When the water falls vertically to the earth as rain, it is considered masculine. Interestingly, almost all of the mountain Apus, or Light Beings, are considered masculine.

Another legend says that the Lake used to be a fertile valley, with the residents living in harmony and happiness. The people were not to go to certain places by order of the Apus. An entity, Auca, told the people that if they went to these places beyond the borders, they would find the flower of fire and they could get the same power as the Apus. So the people didn't obey the Apus. The people left to find the flower of fire. They had been climbing the mountains when the pumas tried to stop them. The people were determined to go on and fought the pumas. Many people died. Father Sun started to cry to see so many of his children dead. Father Sun shed so many tears that the valley became a lake and the people who were left had to live in the mountains nearby.

Yet another legend gives the origin of the name of the Lake. It was said that in the early times, a couple was sailing on the lake in a reed boat. They were saddened to see a number of dead pumas floating on the lake. The pumas were gray in color, so the couple named the lake for the pumas. Titicaca translates to gray puma in Aymara. One of the common beliefs about the name is that the Sacred Rock on Sun Island was called Taypyquala.

This place was considered to be the House of the Sun, the Moon, and the stars. The Incas took pumas to the island to guard the sacred place. The pumas liked the Sacred Rock and would sit on the gray rock all day. Soon, the people started to call the rock, *titiquala* (gray puma). The Island of the Sun was famous and was called Titiquala Island. The people referred to the Lake as the Lake of the Titiquala Island. Later the name became Lake Titicaca.

There are many modern theories about the Lake. One theory is that a glacier engulfed this exact spot, melted, and left a lake over a flowing river. Another popular theory is that the lake was at sea level in ancient, ancient times and rose when the Andes were formed. Supporting this theory is the fact that archeologists have found sea shells imbedded in a possible ancient harbor in the town of Tiawanaku, Bolivia, twenty miles south of Lake Titicaca. Tiawanaku is actually a large area near the lake. The official archeological site is in Bolivia, between the border of Peru and La Paz. This ancient site has many wonders. There are intriguing carved stone heads placed in the stone walls, monoliths, and pyramids near the site of the "harbor."

Modern mysteries are associated with Lake Titicaca. For example, a taxi driver told me one day that he had a fare from the airport in Juliaca to Lake Titicaca. The driver tried to suggest some hotels but the guests, who were foreigners, said they just wanted to go to the Lake. The driver took them to a place on the Lake near Puno. The people got out and paid their fare with a sizable tip. They walked down to the Lake and then strolled along the shore until they were out of sight. The taxi driver thought that they were perhaps taking pictures and sightseeing. Surely they would need a ride to somewhere, he reasoned, so he waited, hoping for the additional fare. The driver waited until after dark. The people never returned. Others claim that there is a UFO landing site at the Lake called Runa Antilis. Many experience energy flowing from the Sacred Lake in all directions. There are strong ley lines that flow from the Lake to other Sacred Sites. It is said that from satellites, the Lake looks like a puma chasing a rabbit.

As a scientific tour guide, I knew a great deal about the lake and the abundance of life living in its waters. The lake has nine groups of native fishes, but the most well-known and largest fish in the lake is the trout. It was introduced to the lake a few decades ago and proceeded to eat the native fishes. From this diet of other fishes, the trout transformed themselves into rainbow trout and are now the most abundant fish in the lake and surrounding rivers. Unlike the rainbow trout from other areas, the flesh of the trout from the lake and its tributaries is pink in color. Jacque

Cousteau explored the depths of Lake Titicaca for submerged cities. His most remarkable discovery was not a lost city, but giant frogs that lived in the depths of the lake and never came to the surface. The folklore is that the some of the frogs of the lake are guardians of treasures that are in the deepest parts of the lake. There is a very large rock near Puno that has the shape of a giant stone frog. When there is a drought, the people collect frogs from the lake and put them on the top of the stone frog to call the rains.

I had heard much of the folklore about Lake Titicaca, but as a young man I was more interested in partying at the festival for the Lady of Candelaria, than in its spiritual meaning. From a gradual process of hearing the legends of the people from different communities on the Lake, I understood the meaning and importance of the Lake in the Andean heritage. Later, I found a reference to the Aymara in the book *Great Messages* by Jorge Raymould de la Feriere. He promotes the theory that the Aymara people are descendents from the Aymaru priest from Mexico, who came to the area looking for the Sacred Lake of their legends. Upon finding the Sacred Lake, they stayed as guardians.

# Ignoring the Heritage

After the mysterious lady left, I did my best to forget all about that day and any meaning that it might have. I was busy being a kid and had little or no interest in any mystical thinking. While I was accustomed to having my mother and uncle respected as yatiris, I had no interest in learning anything about their beliefs or ceremonies. I enjoyed life and was not seeking anything with deeper meaning. I soon forgot about the mysterious lady. As I matured and completed school, my interests did not include metaphysical studies. I wanted to be modern and scientific. I became a tour guide and I loved my work. I was very good at my job and could relate a great deal of information about the heritage of my country and the local sites. Esoteric meanings and Inca legends were far from my everyday reality. That was all to change when I was twenty-five and more mystery entered my life in the form of a magnificent crystal.

# VISITING CRYSTAL

y life was going well. I took pride in my job as a scientific tour guide, and I was happy. The only unusual aspect was that for some reason, most of my clients were mystics and spiritual people. Many of them would give me crystals as gifts. I asked my friends who were tour guides, "Are your clients like that, people with weird ideas and crystals?" They said, "No," and laughed. I started to give the crystals to all of my friends. I didn't need or want them, but people continued to give them to me. It seemed that crystals followed me everywhere. Just when I was completely fed up with crystals, a magnificent crystal came to me. It was unique and beautiful. I loved it. This crystal was not a gift from a client. It came to me in a unique and unusual way. A year and a half later, the crystal was to leave me as mysteriously as it arrived.

# Birthplace of the Incas

s a scientific tour guide, I would tell people, "Lake Titicaca is the highest navigable lake in the world with an altitude of 12,600 feet above sea level and a depth of 1000 feet. It covers 5204 square miles and rests between Bolivia and Peru. There are thirty-two islands on the Lake. Most of them have at least one temple or shrine and are currently inhabited." More important to me now are the Inca beliefs handed down through the centuries. Being the womb of Mother Earth, this Sacred Lake is the place of the creation, the origination. Legend has it that the first Inca and his wife (Manco Capac or Mama Ocllo) emerged from the Lake to help mankind.

Today many tourists visit Sun Island and Moon Island near Bolivia and the islands of Amantani and Taquile, which are in Peru. Near to these two islands are the Reed Islands, called Uros. The Uros people live on islands made up entirely of live reeds. Many of their homes are made of reeds, as are their sailing boats. People have been living on the reed islands for many, many centuries. There are other, less-visited islands. In the deepest part of the Lake is Soto Island, which sits like a natural monument emerging from the deepest waters of the lake. One of the most mysterious islands is Whale Island. There is a legend that says people who go there can disappear into the ether.

There are many legends about the Lake. The natural and mystical beauty of the Lake draws many people to experience its enchantment. That is why the Inca, when he had a quest, would make a pilgrimage to this Sacred Lake, a place considered to be a Cosmic Pedestal. It is not surprising that it was on an island in the Lake that the mysterious crystal would find me and send me on a lifelong quest.

# Encounter with the Crystal

One day, I looked at my schedule and thought that this time I wasn't going to have mystical people on my tour because the tourists were Japanese. I rarely had clients from Japan, not knowing much of their background, I said to myself, finally someone normal. Surprisingly, they were Buddhist monks! They knew of Lake Titicaca and wanted to go to the Sacred Lake. I was stunned, but I quickly hired a boat and we went out on the water. Shortly after we left the shore one of the monks gave me a string of prayer beads. That is when I said, "Okay, this is very incredible. What's going on here?" When we disembarked onto the island of Taquile, I conducted my normal tour. There was some free time for me at mid-day when the tour group was having a picnic lunch. I was very relieved to have time to myself so that I could then be with friends and do what was "normal." I climbed up the steep part of the hill to the house of my friend, Huata, to visit with him for a while. Huata's house has a spectacular view as it overlooks the Lake. I was grateful for the beautiful view of the small harbor and the expanse of deep blue water that stretched for miles. The snow-capped mountains in the background completed the almost unreal picture. But I was in a hurry to talk with my friend, so I kept moving as quickly as possible. Huata's house has a thatched roof, typical of Taquile Island. To my amazement, I immediately noticed a crystal hanging on a chain that was resting on one of the sticks in the roof at the front of the house. This shocked me, so I said to him, "You, too, with the crystals?" "Yes, he said, "but this one is not yours. Yours is inside."

We quickly went inside. I didn't know what he meant when he said that mine was inside. Huata went into another room and brought out a truly magnificent crystal. It was two inches long and shaped like a kaleidoscope. It had a quartz crystal on the bottom. The center was like a silver pipe with three small pink quartz crystals on a band at the bottom of the silver and three small pink quartz crystals on the band at the top of the silver. Positioned in the middle of the silver pipe was a long narrow garnet. Sitting on top of the silver pipe was an amethyst shaped like a heart. The amethyst could rotate, so that you could see through a glass opening in the pipe, moving the quartz at the bottom like a kaleidoscope.

To my great surprise, I was very attracted to this particular crystal. I said, "I like it. I really like it." I wanted to buy the crystal because it was so very, very beautiful. Huata gave it to me saying, "This is yours." I said, "No, no. This is not mine. I have never had anything like this." He said, "A gringo came one day and said somebody's going to ask about a crystal. After many months, you were the first to comment on my crystal, so it is yours." Huata wanted to give me the crystal so that his service would be finished. He said, "I don't need it any further." He no longer wanted to have the responsibility for the crystal.

For some reason, I wanted to buy it. I just wanted to have it. And I said, "Okay." I didn't need this for a special reason. I just wanted it because it was beautiful. I tried to pay for it, but he refused my offer, saying, "I am giving it to you. It is yours." So I said, "Okay, I will accept it but just as a carrier, not as an owner." Later, I was sorry that I accepted it only as carrier. A year and a half later, it disappeared. I always wore the crystal on a silver chain around my neck. I don't know how it disappeared and was astonished to find it gone with no trace. I deeply miss the crystal to this day.

# An Antenna

The first person the crystal attracted was a psychic in Cusco. I was having some coffee with friends at Vara Yoc, a restaurant near the main square in Cusco, when a man with a black beard and mustache approached me. He told me that he knew about the crystal that I was wearing. He told me the crystal was an ancient "power tool" and that it did not belong to this region. He was quite certain that it came from a distant land and that people physically fought for the privilege of carrying this crystal. His belief surprised me, but I did not give much importance to what he said. He gave me his business card. I didn't keep the card and dismissed the entire incident. My friends were concerned that maybe the crystal came from a witchdoctor. I just laughed. All of my friends liked the crystal and thought it was beautiful.

The next encounter with the crystal was with a mystic from Niagara Falls in North America. This man ran a New Age Temple there. He was visiting Sillustani, a Power Place near Puno in the High Plateau. I was there with a small tour group. I was close to one of the *chullpas*, an ancient manmade stone burial tower, explaining the meaning of the tower. This man came to me and asked me about the "tool" that I was wearing. He wanted to use the crystal in a ceremony that he had planned to hold at Sillustani. He invited me to come to the ceremony. I was curious, so I gave my tour group some free time, and went with this mystic and his friends to meditate in a nearby stone circle structure. This man put the crystal in the center of the circle and everyone meditated for about a half hour. It was an interesting experience for me to feel energy anchoring in the crystal resting in the middle of the circle. The mystic said he was using the crystal to send energy to other parts of the world. This was a very different experience for me. I was not accustomed to meditating, and I had never felt the physical force of the energy from an object before.

In my work as a tour guide, I later had a tour group from Finland and all of them were UFO seekers. We went one afternoon to Sillustani and they found the site to be very special. They asked if we could come back during the night and use the crystal as "an antenna." I agreed and we returned to Sillustani that night. One of the people on the tour was in charge of communicating with the UFOs, and he was the one who used the crystal as an antenna. The information he "received" from the UFO was of great interest. The message that night was that the space brothers would be coming later that night and would hover in their spacecrafts at Chilca. This group was disappointed because they said they were unable to go to Chilca due to a previous arrangement. I thought that they were nice people, but I really did not think that they had contacted a UFO. It seemed suspicious that they came to see UFOs but couldn't show up when the "space brothers" said they would be there. Again, I thought I could have a good laugh over my crystal.

# Becoming a Believer

The next day I took a train to Cusco, the main city of the Sacred Valley, with this same group. After we arrived I went for a walk in the main square. I couldn't believe my eyes! The headlines on the front page of a respected Lima newspaper proclaimed, in very big print, that some UFOs had been seen in Chilca the previous night.

Pictures of the space ships were right there on the front page! Incredibly, the information that they received using the crystal as an antenna appeared to be accurate. I walked around Cusco for about an hour trying to make sense of all that had happened since that day in Taquile when I first saw the crystal. Memories of all of the people who were drawn to the crystal came back to me. The comments that I used to laugh at had more importance to me now. It was getting more difficult to ignore the importance of this crystal that I was clutching in my hand.

Walking through Cusco that night, I became convinced that this crystal really could connect with other realities. I was beginning to accept the thought that there existed much more than just what could be experienced with our five senses. Obviously, some things could not yet be explained by science. This incident was evidence for me that there was much to know and explore from esoteric experiences and teachers. Suddenly, I wanted to meet teachers from many traditions. I was now becoming increasingly interested in esoteric or metaphysical pursuits.

# Sillustani

About six months after seeing the picture of the UFOs, I was taking another group to Sillustani. I first told them the factual information about the site. I explained, "Sillustani is a peninsula on Lake Umayo, northwest of Lake Titicaca. It is known as an ancient cemetery. Its main purpose in pre-Incan and Incan times was as a temple, an oracle, a place to understand this life and other lives. If you are lucky, you will find an ancient arrowhead, which dates this spot as being in use in pre-historic times." When my short talk ended, everyone was given free time to explore the area.

I went off on my own and was thinking of how this was a natural spot for UFOs to explore. Sitting near the chullpas you look out over the island sitting in the middle of the lake. The top of the island is flat. It does not take much imagination to visualize it as a "landing pad." On top of the island there are more than sixty circles that are thought to be shrines. This is true of many of the "natural altars" of the High Plateau. Sillustani is special in this regard, since the flat island is surrounded with water.

This particular day, I was curious as to whether or not the island in the lake was a sacred island. The sun was directly overhead and the light danced on Lake Umayu. I closed my eyes for a moment and asked the island to give me some sign that it was truly a sacred island. As I opened my eyes, it was clear that the sun had cast a shadow on the lake of the three steps, three levels of reality, or the symbol of the three worlds of the *chacana*, the Inca Cross. I stood up with a sense of awe and excitement.

This sign was very meaningful to me, so I pointed it out to some of the people on the tour who were sitting nearby. Everyone could see the symbol of the shadow in the water. I then suggested that we walk about fifty feet to the Temple of the Sun, which has three steps into the temple. There once were forty-nine (seven times seven) stones in a circle around the temple. There were twenty-four standing stones on each side with one in the center. This number, forty-nine, is very important in the pre-Incan traditions. For instance there are forty-nine squares of the rainbow colors in the pre-Incan flag, called *wifala*. There is also a legend that forty-nine visitors from three different planets came here to help mankind.

Sillustani is an important Power Place, as is Machu Picchu, for various people. Many people in my tour groups have heard about it. If you look to the west of this island, your view includes an expanse of the High Plateau that transcends the normal, as the light and shadows create a mystical world. The vibrations of Sillustani are also very different. The "veils" between the worlds are very thin, and it feels like you are looking at different realities, as you get lost in the beauty of the light and the landscape.

The Andean tradition holds Sillustani as a site for many temples. The Spanish found tombs and the remains of some human bodies on the site, and thought it to be mainly a cemetery. Local people think of Sillustani as a combination of temple and burial place for special people. In a similar fashion, Christians have cathedrals with popes or bishops buried within the cathedral. The chullpas, towers built of large stones, are regarded as either burial towers or ceremonial towers. They are wider at the top than the bottom, with a band of smaller stones as a headband. I was remembering how beautiful it was when I saw the sun directly overhead, casting a shadow over the chullpa on the ground equally in all directions, which can happen in November and February. This display of equidistant shadowing demonstrates the love of the Father Sun for the Mother Earth in Inca legends. Various symbols are carved into the stones of these towers, leading many people to see them more as initiation places than burial places. Regardless of the beliefs, the chullpas are striking and mysterious.

Whenever I go to Sillustani, even alone, I always feel as if someone is accompanying me and watching me. I sense that it is alive at some other vibration, with a multitude of beings visiting in a mystical gathering place.

# "All Gods and New Faces"

After my encounters with the crystal, I continued my work as a freelance tour guide. Although I was not yet fully immersed in the heritage and metaphysical explanation of the Incas, I was including some of the metaphysical information that I was learning in my work as a guide. Late in September, I was returning to the airport in Juliaca with a group of six people who had just completed a tour of the Region of Lake Titicaca. The driver of the van, Don Pedro, asked me to do him a favor. If I met any people at the airport who were going to Puno, he wanted me to convince them to use his services so he could have a fare for the forty-five minute ride back to Puno. Since I did a lot of work with Don Pedro, I was happy to help him in this way. I noticed two non-Peruvian people standing at the main doorway of the airport. They were apparently waiting for friends who were coming from the baggage claim area. I went over to talk with them to see if they needed transportation to Puno, which is the main destination for tourists in this area. I knew that Don Pedro would be very pleased that I was bringing four passengers back with me to the van.

On the way to Puno the people were very interested in knowing about the floods around the Lake. Normally, it rains 650 milliliters. That year we had more than 1000 milliliters of rain. I explained many of the aspects of the floods and about the area in general. As we approached the city I took the opportunity to offer my services as a tour guide to take them to the islands on the lake. They graciously declined because they were looking for a particular person in Puno. They were expecting to contact this person and have him as a special tour guide. In response I said, "That is okay."

We were now entering the city limits. I said, "Welcome to Puno," and told them the general information. Puno has 130 thousand inhabitants, with a very well-known University, Universidad Macional Del Altiplano, comprising approximately ten percent of the city's population. As I was talking, my curiousity grew concerning the person who was the special tour guide they wanted to contact. Before the end of the trip, I thought that I would ask who they were looking for so that I could help them contact this person. One man opened his notebook and flipped a couple of pages. Imagine my surprise when he said, "His name is Jorge Luis Delgado. Do you know him?" "That is me!" I replied. I could tell that they didn't quite believe me. So I had to show them my ID to prove to them that I was myself.

I recommended that they stay at the Italia Hotel and took them to this hotel in the downtown area. On the way to the hotel, they told me that they were in Peru for some special work and that they would call me that afternoon after they were settled. I was extremely curious by now. It is not usual that people show up wanting to meet me and then my having to prove that I am me. I could hardly wait to know what this was all about.

Late in the afternoon, one of the group members, John Paul, called. I met him and David at a local coffee shop. It turned out that John Paul was from the BBC in London, and David was from the BBC in Wales, Great Britain. Now, I was not only curious, I was excited. Here I was talking to representatives of a well-known international television network. I wondered what they wanted to do here at Lake Titicaca. The first thing I inquired about was how they had heard about me. They told me that I had been recommended by Hellenic Atlantic, a very prestigious travel agency in London. I had been working with this travel agency for some time in Peru as a tour guide. I had even given presentations for them regarding the native textiles and traditions. That mystery solved, I was eager to know what they needed me to do for them.

The BBC had a program called *Everyman.* John Paul and David were here to explore making a documentary film regarding the different religions that were practiced by the people in the area of Lake Titicaca. They proposed that I set up the contacts with the native shamans and Andean priests in different communities around the Lake. They indicated that the purpose of their trip was to set up all of the contacts. They would then return in six months with their crew to film a program titled "All Gods and New Faces." This was the most exciting work that I had ever been offered. Not only would I be working with such an important television network, I would be able to inquire into the Inca beliefs and traditions at a deeper level. It would be necessary to learn a great deal more about the metaphysical aspects of my own heritage to do this work for the BBC. I could not imagine, though, sitting there in the coffee shop, all of the changes that would occur in my life after I spent the next six months learning from the local Aymara yatiris. I did know to say, "Yes, I will do it," immediately. The three of us then spent a few hours together. John Paul and David were eager to learn as much as possible about the Andean people and their culture during the time they had available in Puno.

After this meeting, I constantly prepared for their return. During the week I would be a tour guide. On weekends, I would spend much of my time traveling to various communities and talking to the people and the yatiris. While my personal knowledge was growing, I was also trying to convince some of the yatiris to be a part of the BBC filming. I was met with much reluctance. Most of the yatiris did not want to be filmed. Moviemaking was foreign to them. They had never heard of the BBC, and some of them were fearful that the filming would diminish their "gifts." When John Paul and David returned six months later, we started to interview representatives from the established churches, including the Maryknoll Order of the Catholic Church and the Seventh Day Adventists. Of course, they also wanted to interview people who practiced the native Inca traditions. I explained that many of the indigenous people practiced Inca traditions and also belonged to the Catholic religion. For example, many yatiris have the crucifix on their mesa, or altar, with their native Inca symbols and power tools. Since John Paul and David were so insistent on filming a yatiri, I went again to ask a local yatiri to participate. His name was Natalio Silva.

# Not on Tuesday

t took a lot of talking to convince Natalio to participate in the film. The film was carefully planned since the film crew was only to be in Peru a short time. Each day of filming was now planned and scheduled. The first day was to be about the local crops, for example. On Tuesday we went to meet Natalio at his community, Yanamur, at a prearranged time. When we arrived at his house, his wife ran out of the house calling a greeting. She told me that we had a little problem. "Natalio is not here. He is in jail!" she said in a breathless voice. "What happened?" I asked. "Last night he went to the town and after some drinks, some of his compadres were fighting. He tried to stop them, and the police came and took everybody who was there to jail." We went to the van and quickly drove a couple of miles to the local town to see if we could get Natalio out of jail. When we arrived at the police station, we spoke to the police officer and explained that we were with the BBC and that we were working with the yatiris and needed Natalio Silva's assistance.

In a booming voice, the officer called out "Natalio Silva." A short time later Natalio marched in from the back of the jail. He said to the officer, "Yes, Sir!" in military fashion. The officer said, "Your friends are here so you can go." It is possible that the large cameras the crew carried helped convince the officer to allow Natalio to leave. Natalio did not seem anxious to leave with us. After a moment Natalio said, "You see, I didn't want to work on

Tuesday. Thank you for coming for me but I am not working today. I will see you tomorrow." We could not change his mind. After all, he had gotten himself arrested and spent the night in jail so as not to work on Tuesday.

I convinced the crew to change the daily schedule. We went to film the birds of Lake Titicaca. We spent part of the day filming the Andean flamingo which lives all year round on the Lake and nests only in this area. Fortunately, everyone was pleased with the filming that day. I was anxious the next morning as we went, yet again, for Natalio. It was now even more important that he be ready to make the film. Natalio was ready and in a very happy mood when we met him in front of his house on Wednesday. I asked why he would not work on Tuesday. All he said was that in the tradition, Tuesday was not a good day for the work of the yatiris. Some yatiris also would not work on Friday, but for him it was only Tuesday. He did not want to say he wouldn't work on Tuesday after he agreed to be in the film. Instead he landed in jail!

# Reed Islands

Natalio rode in a medium-sized reed boat to reach the Reed Islands. Normally, this boat would be used for fishing and could hold two people. The boats are made entirely of reeds that are called *totora*. The people propel the boats with paddles or just the rudder. The islands are about two miles to the closest shore of Lake Titicaca. There are actually forty inhabited reed islands of different sizes. This is a kind of Totora civilization, because they eat the roots of the totora. They build their houses with totora and use dried totora for fuel. Their transportation is on reed boats. They also make their mattresses of totora. This reed has good insulation from heat and cold, as well as comfort for the people. When it rains the totora swells and keeps the rain from entering the reed houses. They also sell reed boats and other handicrafts to acquire money to buy needed commodities. For centuries these people have lived on these islands. It is said that the ancestors of the Uros culture lived on the reed islands before the "birth of the sun" in the ancient dark ages. There are many legends about these people. They have remained quite isolated from other communities, but in today's world, many of the children now travel daily to the mainland for secondary school. The primary schools are still on the islands.

Since this community is so interesting and unique, I thought that this would be a very good place to film Natalio and his work. Natalio's primary work this day was to heal a lady on the island. In order to "diagnose" her problem, Natalio worked with a guinea pig that he had brought with him from his kitchen (guinea pigs are raised for food throughout the highlands of the Andes). Natalio performed a ceremony asking the Apus and Pachmama to help us. He read the coca leaves to ascertain the correct moment to start his work. He also read in the coca leaves that the sickness was inside the lady and that he would need to work with the guinea pig. He then had the lady put the guinea pig under her shirt in contact with her skin. Natalio then sacrificed the guinea pig in order to view the sickness that, according to native beliefs, transferred to the guinea pig. The guinea pig revealed that the lady had a problem with her liver. Natalio gave the lady some herbs and promised to send more when he went to the market. She was to take the herbal infusion daily for several weeks. He also suggested that the lady make a paste of special clay, chaco, and put it on her stomach over her liver.

The BBC crew was able to film one of the native traditions of healing in the area of Lake Titicaca. The crew was happy with the filming and enjoyed their day on the Reed Islands. As their work was completed, John Paul, David and their crew departed for England shortly after this day with Natalio. The experience had left me with new friends in the BBC and also many close relationships with the local yatiris in numerous communities around the Lake.

# Ruben Cederño

After working with the BBC, I went back to my normal work as a tour guide. However, now I was continuing to learn more about the Inca traditions and beliefs. I was no longer a strictly scientific tour guide. As fate would have it, I was to have yet another interesting encounter at the airport in Juliaca, when I met a metaphysical teacher, Ruben Cederño. Again, I was taking people to the airport. Some local workers had called a strike, or work stoppage, for that day. Usually, during a strike, the workers put a lot of large rocks on the roadways to stop people from going to or from the airport. So we left very early, by five o'clock in the morning to get our small group on a ten o'clock airplane flight. We joined another tour group in a small bus. While we were talking and socializing, a man from Venezuela joined the conversation. He looked like a person from India rather than Venezuela and spoke in an elegant fashion. This man seemed to be very learned and I was drawn to him. He was a musician with a great deal of knowledge of this field and this culture. I felt a great resonance with him. Before we left the bus for the airline, he gave me a little book about metaphysics and told me that his name was Ruben Cederño.

The book discussed the Ascended Masters in the Andes. This information was new to me. The book mentioned Arama Muru and Amara Mara becoming the god and goddess, Meru. I saw that it was one of the metaphysical teachers connected with the magic of the Lake. Ruben said that the most important place on the planet was Lake Titicaca because it is the focus of the feminine polarity of the planet. I had heard about this concept before, but the way that Ruben was expressing it felt like it truly came from his heart. The only reason Ruben was in Peru was to be at the Lake, and to expand his information about the god and goddess. After some weeks I went to Le Paz, Bolivia. In the window of a large bookstore were many books with the name Ruben Cederño as the author. The books talked about Christ and many topics surrounding the Ascended Master.

# Condori

All of this information was very interesting to me. Why had I not heard of this before? I started to ask people I knew who were interested in metaphysics, if they knew of any of this. No one in Cusco, or near Machu Picchu and the North, knew of these concepts. When I started to ask in the communities around Lake Titicaca, I found a few yatiris in the Highlands who knew of some legends. It was in Acora, a region near the Lake with a small village also named Acora, about forty miles from the Bolivian border, that I met Condori, a yatiri from the village.

The first time that I invited Condori to work as a yatiris and do a ceremony for one of my tour groups was full of surprises. The first surprise came when the tour bus came to the place near the road where we were to meet Condori. It was early in the morning, a little after sunrise. We came to the designated place and stopped the bus. It was a big bus because we had a group of about eighteen German tourists and were going to the beach for a native ceremony. I waited for a few moments with growing anxiety, for Condori was nowhere in sight. Then I noticed something a few yards down the road. I was not sure what was there. I went out to see what it was or if I could see Condori in the distance on his way to the bus. As I got closer to the form on the side of the road I recognized that it was someone asleep, leaning on a large bundle. Of course it was Condori. I went over and gently shook him to awaken him. I asked him if he was okay. "Yes," he replied, "I spent the entire night with the Spirits preparing for the ceremony and then I fell asleep waiting for the bus." I wondered what spirits he was communing with. We quickly went to the bus and proceeded to the beach. When we got to the beach, Condori opened his large bundle, wrapped in a very strong fibrous native paper. Inside the paper was a large modern suitcase containing all of his ceremonial belongings. Despite our unusual beginning, Condori conducted a traditional ceremony to Mother Earth, and the tour group participated with enthusiasm. Everyone seemed to be in a relaxed mood, and we had many laughs together that day.

During the return trip on the bus I took the opportunity to ask Condori if he had ever heard of Aramu Muru of the Golden Disc. Condori said that he knew about a Master who brought the Golden Disc from far away to this continent. The Golden Disc was kept for some period of time in Tiawanaku, Pucara, and Cusco. For some unknown reason, all these sacred sites are aligned and equidistant on the ley line (earth energy lines) that people know as The Road of Wiracoccha. Condori said that wherever the Golden Disc was kept, there was great development in the people's culture and expansion of their consciousness. That is why the Disc was considered a gift and was protected by the Incas. When the Spaniards arrived, the Incas knew in advance that foreigners would be arriving. Consequently, as soon as it was confirmed that the Spanish were on this continent, the Incas took the Golden Disc and put it into the depths of Lake Titicaca for safekeeping until the New Sunrise.

This confirmation of legends in the Inca traditions was important to me because it gave some local Incan testimony to support some of the metaphysical beliefs of Ruben. There is not much mentioned in books about Aramu Muru and the Golden Disc, but this information resonated in my heart. It was on this basis that later I would know in my heart that it was Aramu Muru that I saw entering the Doorway that morning at Willca Uta.

My scientific mind was still strong and ever present, but I realized that now I was also listening with my heart to a different kind of knowing. This new dimension of understanding or consciousness was ever growing in intensity. As much as I had avoided my spiritual and cultural heritage when

I was a boy and very young man, I was becoming passionate in my thirst for all that was Inca. Sometimes, my scientific mind would challenge my experiences. Other times, it felt like the knowing from my mind and the knowing from my heart were in balance. One thing that I was certain of on all levels was that the direction of my life had been permanently changed from the moment I saw that magnificent, kaleidoscope crystal.

# DANCING FIRE PEOPLE

was so excited to have my own tour company and open a new office that I almost forgot to put the message on the radio for Antonio to come and give the blessing. Antonio was from the Paratia community, which is a very cold region in the mountains outside of Puno. Paratia was at the time quite inaccessible and over the centuries had little impact from outside influences. There were no phones in the community. The only way to reach Antonio was to put a message on a certain radio station. The only transportation for the two-day trip was to travel by truck and then complete the remainder of the journey on foot. The name Paratia means "land where the rain never stops." I didn't have the time to go to the community, but I felt confident that if I put a message on the radio with the time and the place, Antonio, or some other yatiri from the community, would come. I liked Antonio so I was very hopeful that he would be able to come to this celebration and conduct a ceremony.

I admired many things about this community. I have a passion for textiles, and the Paratia are considered to have the purest lineage of the Inca textiles and traditions, with sophisticated designs of the Father Sun and Mother Earth. I was remembering my first visit to Paratia, during fiesta time. There are still not many visitors to the community, although the opening of a mine has brought more people to the area. To this day, though, their traditions and fiestas are unique and a pure continuation of the Inca ways. The music reflects a solemn feeling of a sacred procession. The instruments are panpipes and drums that intone a singular beat, reflecting the rhythm of the heart. The musicians told me that their music awakens something from deep inside your heart and connects you with the Cosmos.

In contrast to this solemnity, the male dancers wear large headdresses made from plumes of the South American ostrich, Rea. These large plumes are white and brown and believed to connect the wearers with their ancestors back to ancient times. The dancers also wear black jackets with many bold colored buttons sewn in intricate patterns on the front of the jacket and on the sleeves and cuffs of the calf-length black pants. The men wear a white cloak trimmed in red over their shoulder. The dancers also carry a drum to their left side and hold the panpipes with their right hand close to their chest. On their backs hang a banner with many mirrors and colorful tassels. To complete their homemade outfit, they wear a coca bag with many levels of pearl-like beads and tassels of different colors. The music and dancing continues all day and into the night for two days.

# Antonio

My friend in Puno, Maria, first introduced me to Antonio when she had him come to her home for a special ceremony. I was very impressed by how I was moved emotionally during the ceremony connecting us with the Mother Earth. I talked with Antonio a lot that day. He invited me to come to the Paratia community for the fiesta. I asked around and found out that Antonio was a very well-known *paq'o*, which is Quechua for Andean priest. His specialty was making offerings to the Mother Earth and the Apukunas or Mountain Spirits.

It was difficult to say how old Antonio really was. His energy was very young, but he was probably in his fifties. His wisdom, though, was very "old," like a wise grandfather. He presented himself and his beliefs as very "simple" and uncomplicated. This was because he was so grounded in his wisdom and habits. Like most of the Paratia, Antonio was a herder of alpacas and llamas. Herding is the main occupation of most of the people living in this mountain region. Antonio was average to small in physical stature, but his presence seemed to expand when he talked about the Andean cosmology and the Inca beliefs. He was married, and this union led to much respect and many responsibilities in the community. In most of the Andean communities, only married people can vote. Married men must take on the responsibility of being the mayor or community leader for a year. Another year, he will be in charge of the fiesta. The belief in these communities is that only married people are prepared to handle these positions of responsibility, and that everyone must take a turn in handling these community duties while also taking care of their families.

Antonio's house was made of stone and adobe bricks, with a thatched roof. There were three rooms, each two by three yards in size. Each room had a window and combined adobe bricks with open space. One of the rooms had seats around it, and Antonio said that this was the "male" room and that the kitchen was the "female" room. Even in the house, Antonio had the polarities. There were adobe walls surrounding the house that secured the dogs, the guinea pigs, and a few chickens. Surrounding the house were pastures bordered by small walls of adobe, where the llamas and alpacas were kept in the nighttime. Their dung was then used to fertilize the fields where the family grew potatoes and *quinua*, a high protein grain.

Potatoes are the main staple in the diet of the High Plateau, so the potato is a very important crop. In the Andes, the only harvest time for the various crops is following the rainy season of December thru March, in April and May. The potatoes need to be stored for the entire year. The people from pre-Incan times would dehydrate the potatoes, so the potatoes would last in an edible state for four or five years. One only had to soak them in water overnight to re-hydrate them. The Paratia Community had the perfect conditions to dehydrate or "freeze dry" their potato crops. The people would soak the potatoes in water and leave them high in the mountains to freeze overnight in May and June. They would leave them soaking in the freezing water for one week and then put them out to dry in the sun for a second week. The potatoes were ready to store until they were needed. In the Highlands, the people grow many types of potatoes. Some are small, round, and black. I particularly enjoy them in potato soup. There are finger-like small sweet potatoes with yellow skins that are very delicious. In all, there are almost three hundred kinds of potatoes are grown in Peru.

# Community Life

During my visit, Antonio had to attend to some business. I had taken this time to walk in the two village squares to observe the activities of the people. Since many families from the surrounding mountain communities were in Puno for the festival, many local inhabitants set out their products to sell and trade in the main square where the small chapel stood. Common to Catholic communities, the church would be located in the main square. On the opposite side of the square, there were cloths on the ground with colorful mixtures of fresh vegetables and many varieties of potatoes. Even the people from the outlying communities brought their products at this time. Many brought wool and skins from the llamas and alpacas, but these were displayed in the other square, which adjoins the main square. Both are similar in size. It was in the second square that I recognized a lady who Antonio had introduced to me earlier in the day.

Rosario was one of the village weavers. I was very impressed with her work. As in most of the Andean communities, she used a horizontal loom made of sticks and picked up the stitches with a llama bone. Rosario designed the fabric in an ancient manner that can be traced back to the Paracas people, who were a pre-Incan civilization. The uniqueness of the Paratia textiles is that the pattern of the design is woven into both sides of the textile. One side is more beautiful and more finished looking, but the other side has the full design. The textile is reversible. While I was visiting the home of a friend in the United States, I immediately noticed a textile that was prominently hung in the main foyer. Being a collector of textile in the Andes, I thought that I was looking at one of the designs of the Paratia. Upon examining the textile, at my friend's invitation, I was more confident that it originated in this Inca community. The design was woven on both sides, with one side being more predominant. I was really shocked when my friend said that the textile had come from Bali. It is a mystery of how unique, yet similar, the textiles of two people from two different parts of the world can be.

Rosario was not at her loom, but in the square. She had set up a table with an umbrella and was selling food. I stopped and chatted with her. I decided to have some food, since Antonio had not yet returned and I was hungry. The food smelled wonderful and, like most Andean people, I love to eat good food! I was not disappointed with the alpaca, potatoes, and noodles in a chili sauce with lettuce that Rosario served me in a large soup bowl, as is the custom in the High Plateau. I finished my meal and walked around the square, still waiting for my friend to return.

Time seems to be elastic here. A few moments can easily turn into an hour or longer. These people, who are shy with outside visitors, appear to walk in another dimension of time. I try to live in the moment, but these people seem to suspend the moment. For the Paratia, nothing is more important than what you are doing or whom you are speaking with at that moment. I don't think that these apparently happy people could even comprehend the feeling of stress. They truly seem to ignore time and there is never a sense of hurry or distress. All scheduled events are approximations and there is much patience with each other's individual schedules. The result is a very noticeable harmony shared by the people. Children roamed freely everywhere in the village. They were so happy with each other and filled the air with laughter. I noticed two young sisters, about the ages of five and six years, walking hand in hand into the square. They swung their clenched hands and arms high in the air in delight. Nowhere in this small village of about forty permanent families did I see disharmony. This was also true of the families from the communities scattered throughout the mountains who had come to Paratia for the festival.

My friend, Antonio, returned and said that his business was complete and we would have the rest of the day together. When I told him of my observations about the people, he confirmed my observances and said, "People here are all very happy in their family life and with everyone in the community. Each of the visiting mountain communities is really an extended family. Everyone cares for the other. There is no need for police or any other outside control. We all rely on one another and live happily together. There is a very regular life here, so time is quite unimportant to us. Of course, the animals are considered part of the family, and you will find equal harmony between the people and the animals. We have happy animals too," Antonio added with a laugh.

Antonio said that there was going to be a *despacho* (ceremonial offering) this afternoon in the courtyard behind the mayor's office to begin the festival. I asked if he was performing the ceremony. He explained that they had two Apus, and that they always communicated with each other. For this reason, every offering had to have an offering to each Apu. Furthermore, two paq'os, one male and one female, performed all ceremonial offerings held in the village. Today their ceremony would be performed by the paq'o, Paq'o. I guess I had a puzzled expression on my face, because Antonio burst into laughter. "Yes, the paq'o's name is Paq'o," he said as he continued to laugh. "Come," he said, "Let's go and meet Paq'o and his wife, who will be performing the ceremony with him." As Antonio got up to leave I asked, "Is his wife's name Paq'o, too?"

Antonio just laughed and patted me on the back as we walked toward the village offices across the square. When I met Paq'o and his wife (I cannot remember her name, but it wasn't Paqo), we all had a good laugh together. Paq'o had been trained to be a paq'o from a very early age by his grandfather. His grandfather wanted Paq'o to follow in his footsteps as a paq'o, so he may have been intended to be a paq'o since birth. Antonio and Paq'o explained that the traditions were handed down through the families. You became recognized as a powerful paq'o only by being accepted as such by the people, or by being struck by lightening. I personally would prefer the first method!

Every community in the Andes has their own particular traditions concerning the offerings or despacho. There are slightly different ceremonies if you are making an offering to an Apu or to Pachamama. Within the community traditions, there are still individual differences in how each paq'o or yatiri conducts their despacho or offering. In Paratia that day, Paq'o and his wife performed an offering to the two Paratia Apus. Paq'o wore a festive poncho with no hat for the ceremony. His wife was dressed beautifully in her fiesta garb. She wore a multicolored wool skirt and a black jacket with the entire bodice covered with brilliant colored buttons sewn into a unique design. She had a multicolor, multi-designed shawl around her shoulders. Most impressive was her wide brimmed hat. The hat was black, but you hardly noticed its color, as your eyes were drawn to the encircling fringe of hanging pearl-like beads ending in a bright red tassel. The top of the crown of the hat was covered in a design of colorful buttons. Her costume, traditional for the women, was distinctive and stunning in harmony with the costumes of the fiesta dancers.

The ceremony began with the traditional kintuis, containing each person's intentions. Each participant blows their individual wish or intention onto the kintui and offers it to each of the Apus. The kintui for the second Apu was dipped in wine and a local alcohol, but not for the first Apu. I was particularly curious about the bell on a cord with many small objects that Paq'o held in his hand during the ceremony. After the ceremony was completed in the courtyard (it would be burnt at a later time), I asked Paq'o about the significance of the bell and the objects. The bell was to call the Apus. One of the objects was hand carved from alabaster. I had a collection of such hands as objects of Andean art, but did not understand the meaning the paq'os attached to them. Accompanying the bell on the cord were crystal beads and beautiful stones. I was told that they came from India and were used in ancient times as a rosary. Paq'o explained that they were symbols of power. Since his was very old and handed down to him, it contained a great deal of power. My meeting with the Paq'o, seemed like a re-encounter with inherent knowledge. I felt welcomed and at home with the traditions of the Paratia Community.

# Pacha

t was late the following afternoon, after the animals had returned from their grazing in the mountains, that Antonio and I sat a little ways from his house and started the first of many conversations about the Cosmos and the heritage of our ancestors. One very interesting concept he taught me was that *Pacha* is not only space and time. Pacha also includes quantity, other realities, the Divinity, even what is still a mystery. Pacha, explained in a simple or narrow way, is comprised of three worlds. There is the *Uku Pacha* or Underground World represented by the Snake. *Kay Pacha* is the Middle World of this reality, represented by the puma. Then there is *Hanan Pacha* or the Upper World of the Light Beings, represented by the condor.

# Chewing Coca Leaves

Antonio opened his bag of coca leaves, chose three of the best shaped leaves, and placed them on top of each other slightly spread apart and formed a kintui. Antonio blew his intention of honoring the Mother Earth on the coca leaves and then crumbled them into dust as an offering to Mother Earth. He said in a calling voice, "Let's chew, Pachamama. Let's chew, beloved Pachamama." When people are socializing in the Andes they usually offer each other coca leaves as a symbol of friendship and sharing. So it is normal to be chewing coca leaves during a visit or during a conversation. It is polite and an expression of hospitality. There is even a ceremony in the giving and receiving of the coca leaves. Coca leaves are offered with one hand. However, it is a sign of respect to receive them with both hands, or placed in your hat, your bag for coca leaves, or in the corner of the poncho. It is considered impolite to receive them in one hand. These are very ancient customs.

We sat for a while chewing coca leaves mixed with some lliqta which is made of quinua and other plant ashes. Antonio was remembering how things were changing. Now we call Mother Earth by the names of Pachamama or Mamapacha. But his grandfather told him that in the old times, Pachamama was Mother Earth. Mamapacha was the name for the Cosmic Mother. When we talk about Pachamama, we are also connecting to Uku Pacha, the Underground World. But this world is not a very well-known dimension. It is an unknown world with much hidden information and mystery. The animal that represents Uku Pacha in the Andean tradition is Amaru, the Snake.

# Uku Pacha

Antonio asked me if I ever saw any old-looking snakes in my life. I said, "No." He said, "You never will see an old snake, because the snake is always shedding its skin." That is what we ask from the Snake. We ask him to teach us how to shed our skins of pain, fear, sorrow, and guilt like he sheds his skin. I said to Antonio, who is a Quechua paq'o, "In my native Aymara tradition, this underground world is called Mancca Pacha, because Mancca means to eat. It is named for an aspect of the Mother Earth that eats." Antonio replied, "Right! That's correct! It is the Mother Earth who is always ready to help us, releasing our heavy energies. It is for this purpose we use coca leaves, flower petals, and incense in a special ceremony to carry our wishes or intentions with our requests and our messages to the Mother Earth."

Then Antonio asked me if I knew of the other "energies" or "beings" that live in the Underground World. "Are you talking about the energies who live deep in the mines who guard the veins of the silver and gold?" I answered. Antonio replied, "Yes! These energies like to 'eat and drink' a lot. We often have ceremonies offering coca leaves and chicha to live in harmony with these energies." Antonio was very pleased that I had this knowledge of the Uku Pacha, because there is much wisdom to gain from the Underground World. He then offered me more coca leaves to chew.

"In some of our pilgrimages, we go into the caves in the mountains. We do this because we know that these places can receive the heavy energies through the intentions on the coca leaves. The Mother Earth will take care of these energies. The Mother Earth can transmute any heavy energy. Nothing is too difficult for her. She easily takes dark matter and turns it into a beautiful crystal." I then told Antonio about my crystal that looked like a kaleidoscope and could be used as a power tool. He was very interested in all of my experiences and felt that the crystal had been sent to me for a period of time so that I would be drawn to the knowledge of the Inca ways. Antonio ended the conversation saying, "Nothing happens by accident."

# Kay Pacha

The sun was setting and the temperature was dropping. We went into the house and got ready for the dinner that Antonio's wife was preparing for us. We enjoyed a delicious corn soup and *quispiño*. Quispiño is like a large dumpling that is cooked in water flavored with different highland grasses. The dumpling is formed in the palm of the hand and keeps its shape even after it is cooked. Quispiños will last for many days after they are cooked. The Paratia people keep quispiños like others would keep and serve bread. We took time to enjoy the food and only talked about everyday matters.

After the meal, the conversation continued about the worlds of the Pacha. This world, the world of our experiences, is called the Kay Pacha. Antonio said, "This world is a manifestation of another reality that exists in the Cosmos. This is the place where we remember 'who we are'." I asked him what he meant by this. He said, "We have a saying in Quechua, *Taripay Pacha*, which means the time to find ourselves. We are in this reality of experience to recognize our entire being in our heavy energies (sorrows and regrets), our gifts, and the Essence of where we originated. According to our ancestors, our Father is the Sun, so we are the Children of the Sun."

He continued, "This means that it is our heritage that everything comes from the Light. All that comes from the Light is alive. And if it is alive, it has vibrations. According to how dense the vibration is, indicates the different levels of reality or frequency. But this Kay Pacha is interconnected with the different worlds. It is manifested in the beauty and perfection of all created things. All of the reality of the experience of Kay Pacha is one in the Essence. We are here to experience this creation, not to judge ourselves. We need to release our heavy energies. We have the opportunity to develop and manifest our unique gifts and dreams in this reality. It is important to understand who you are, so that you can begin to realize that you are one with the Cosmos."

"This is the World of the Puma," I said. Antonio smiled in agreement and he asked me if I was a puma. All I could say at the time was, "I don't know." Anthony then said, "There is a lot of Puma Runa, the Puma People, coming to Mother Earth at this time. The Puma Runa are coming with the new Cycle, the new Sunrise, the PachaKuti. The puma means many things to the Quechua. The puma is a warrior. The puma has balance. The puma has purpose. The Puma Runa have these same qualities in their spiritual quest as they experience all the Worlds and their realities. A potential puma lives in every person." Antonio then said, "You know, the puma walks alone. So part of our spiritual journey is alone. We can do special ceremonies together. We can pray together. But there are some things only you can do on your own. Only you can bring the heavy energies from inside of you.

"The great teaching of the puma is that it is the animal with the least ego; the puma never seeks to be seen. The puma does what he needs to do to survive without calling attention from anybody. You don't see the puma. You only see the results of where he has been." I commented, "Yes, in all of the Andes I think that the puma is recognized for these things, but I never thought about how important the puma's qualities related to walking the spiritual path in quite this way. You have given me much to think about." "Remember also," Antonio said, "that Kay Pacha is the World in which the Children of the Sun must learn to live by the Inca Laws. But that is another conversation." It was getting late, but I said, "We can't stop now. What about the Hanan Pacha, the Upper World?"

# Hanan Pacha

Antonio laughed and said, "Okay, we will finish, but first we will have a little chicha." About a half hour later Antonio resumed the conversation about Pacha. "My grandfather told me that there was more than one Upper World. But now we will talk of Hanan Pacha, the World of the Light, the World of Divinity." "Is that why the symbol of the Upper World is the Condor from the Con Energy, or the Divine Force of Light Energy?" I asked. "Of course," Antonio said as he sipped the chicha. "It is also why there are the legends of Master Teachers. It is in the reality of the Apukunas. The Condor is our messenger from the Cosmos and connects the reality of the Light Beings to this reality.

"When the Spaniards arrived they told us about the angels, the saints, and the Master Jesus. The Master Jesus is also considered to reside in the Hanan Pacha in connection to us and the Divine. The Children of the Sun found it natural to accept these beliefs about these Light Beings who live in the reality of the vast and multileveled Upper World." I had always heard of the Hanan Pacha, but I never had it explained to me in this manner. What I really wanted to know was how to make contact with the Upper World of the Apukunas and other Light Beings. So I just asked Antonio, "Do you make contact or communicate with the Hanan Pacha?"

Antonio said, "Yes. The key is opening your heart." "Okay," I replied, "How do you open your heart?" "Practice ayni with all people and all of nature," was his quick reply. I wanted to know more about the deeper meaning of ayni and other Inca beliefs, but at this time I was more interested in the Upper World. After contemplating these things quietly for a while, I asked, "How do you know when your heart is open?" "Ah," he said with an intriguing smile. "You will know." With these words Antonio ended the conversation. Seeing the disappointment in my face, Antonio added, "The understanding and deeper meaning of ayni and the essence of the Inca beliefs will unfold for you in the right moment and in the right place. For now, this is enough." These prophetic statements were my only comfort while the ideas and questions raced through my mind as I tried to sleep that night.

# The Condor Soars

I t was a few years later that the words spoken that night at Antonio's were finally real to me. I was taking an American tour group with spiritual interests to Machu Picchu as I had done so many times before. This time, things were to be different in many ways. It was October and the weather mild. The spring rains had not started yet. There were some showers, but they passed quickly. You could clearly see the valleys and the Snow Mountains with all the Apus. We were the only group at Machu Picchu this evening. The tourists had left and, with special permission, we were able to go back to this historic site to hold our ceremonies in this mystical Power Place. We had been at Machu Picchu for four days, but this was the group's first visit at night. The sky was clear and you could easily see the Milky Way. Everybody was feeling the presence of the Spirits.

It seemed that everyone in the group of about twenty-five people had gone deep inside themselves. The magic of the night induced a reverent silence. I was aware of the rhythm of my heart. We spent four hours in the Sanctuary of Machu Picchu. We had time for group meditations and free personal time. At approximately one o'clock in the morning, I called everyone to regroup at a pre-set place so that we could all depart together. We met in an open area to the left of the great stone that faces Putu Cusi, the "Always Flowering" or "Always Happy" Mountain.

Everyone sat in a circle. I was seated facing the East. My body felt very relaxed as I closed my eyes. In a commanding voice, I started to call the different native names for the Divinity, invoking the assistance of the Apus and Pachamama. "ILLA-TECSE-CAYLLA-MUYOC-APU-KONTIKI-WIRACOCHAN-PACHAYACHACHEC-PACHACAMAC." As I was calling the names of the Divinity, I started to hear the sound of the wings of the Condor. I thought that I was only thinking in my mind, but I actually said aloud, "The Condor is coming!" One member in the group asked, "Who did you say was coming?" I said, "The Condor is coming." With eyes still closed, I pointed with my right hand in the direction from which it was approaching. Then somebody said "Whoa, whoa." Then I opened my eyes. There was a huge cloud with a clear shape of the condor moving his wings and slowly approaching us. It was a moment of joy. Many of us had tears in our eyes. We closed the ceremony with many hugs, as we felt bonded in a very unique mystical experience.

Some days later, I talked with a local teacher about this experience. He said, "The Condor always was there. You could not see it because your heart was not yet opened." More tears came to my eyes as I remembered Antonio's words, "You will know," when I asked him how to open my heart at his house in Paratia. I knew in my own heart that I had made contact with Hanan Pacha.

# Office Blessing

I have many fond memories of the role that Antonio played in my growing passion for the spiritual. Throughout the years, more and more people came to Peru seeking a more spiritual rather than a strictly scientific tour guide. Now I had my own Tour Company called Kontiki and was opening my first office. The name of the tour company has significance. I was on my way back from some of the islands on the Lake as a free-lance tour guide. I had gone up to the top of the tour boat and was meditating to pass the time. During the meditation, an idea, or message, came to me to open an office for people to be able to contact me to be their tour guide. I wanted to attract people who wanted spiritual or mystical experiences at our many Power Places, in addition to seeing the sights as a tourist. I wanted to take people to "alive" places instead of "ruins," because I knew that all of these sites are energized.

Three names came to me during the meditation. They were Tunupa, yatiris, and *kontiki*. Tunupa is a name of a "Master or Light Being," who came from Lake Titicaca. His face is carved in the side of the mountain at Ollantaytambo in the Sacred Valley of the Incas. Yatiri is the Aymara name for an Andean priest. Kontiki comes from "kon," Divine Energy, and "tiki," Earth Energy. Kontiki signifies the connection of the two energies. I decided to use Kontiki for the name of my travel company. Now that I had the office, I was looking forward to the blessing ceremony and family celebration of my new venture.

The morning of the festivities, I was remembering the day I went to the Alacitas, a once-a-year market in Puno in early May, where many people displayed miniatures of all aspects of life. The tradition is that you purchase a miniature representing what you wish for in the following year. Many miniatures are replicas of things, such as houses, offices, crops, animals, etc. Other people sell miniatures of licenses, diplomas, and other official documents such as passports and visas. Everywhere there are packets of miniature money that all the people hope for, as well as miniature crops for a good harvest. Last year, on the third of May, I had purchased a miniature office and went to the chapel to have my wish or intention blessed. At the chapel, the traditional large cross was painted a primary green that you see throughout the High Plateau. Many paq'os and yatiris , as well as Catholic priests, are present, as well as Catholic priests, for the blessings. Most people have their intentions blessed by both. I was thinking that next year I would purchase a miniature hotel and have my intention blessed in the same way. Antonio arrived the day before the ceremony. I was very happy to see him and grateful that he was able to come. The next day, we had the blessing of the office at two o'clock in the afternoon. All of my family and many friends were there to share the results of my hard work and good fortune. The despacho consisted of dried fruits, candies, and other tin symbols to send messages to Mother Earth There was confetti and colorful ribbons in all of the rainbow colors in the despacho. The ceremony took approximately three hours. After we finished, Antonio offered individual cleansings and asked for blessings for all of us. It was a wonderful ceremony and had great meaning to everyone who attended.

Antonio honored me by having me carry the despacho from the office to my house. Despachos are to be burned or buried so that the intentions and messages go to Mother Earth and the Mother can fulfill the blessings. Antonio "read" the coca leaves and said that the offering had to be burned in the middle of the night.

# The Initiation

At my house, my wife provided a small buffet of traditional foods for my family and friends. Many people decided to remain for the burning of the despacho to complete the ceremony. Antonio said that he would like to have a drink. I went and found a bottle of pisco, an alcoholic drink made from grapes. We made some pisco sours, a very delicious and popular drink in Peru. We all enjoyed chewing coca leaves and drinking pisco sours. I was surprised when after two drinks, Antonio was in a very sound sleep and it was impossible to wake him. We decided to let him sleep until the middle of the night when we were to complete the ceremony. A couple of hours later everyone thought that it was the correct time to finish the ceremony. Again we tried to awaken Antonio. I thought that after a couple of hours sleep he would be revitalized. He would not awaken no matter how hard we tried to arouse him.

What was I to do? Everyone was ready to go home, and they told me that I should proceed with the ceremony. I decided to accept their suggestion since I had attended this type of ceremony many times. I did know the procedure the paq'o usually used to close the ceremony of a "blessing." I did the traditional *challa*. This is an offering that we perform by putting wine into a shell and throwing offering outward to Pachamama in the direction of the sun, first to the right side, and then to the left side of the place for the burning of the despacho. We then repeated this ceremony with pisco. We created an enclosed area with some stones and filled it with cow dung. We lit the dung and placed the entire offering on the burning dung until it was consumed in the fire. It is important that the entire despacho is completely burned.

In the Andes, most houses have a place designated for burning of ceremonial despachos. It is usually marked or identified by a rock that is thought to be sacred to the family. In some areas, people do not like you to watch the despacho as it burns. Nobody likes to be watched when they eat. The people do not think that you should watch Mother Earth as she eats the offering. However, since I was doing the ceremony, I had to check to see how the despacho was burning.

When I went and looked at the burning offering, I saw a ring of fire. I stood there for a moment in the darkness thinking about how the day had unfolded. I had never expected to be the one doing the ceremony. I had to admit to myself that I had felt surprisingly comfortable performing the rituals even with my family and friends watching me. It was a bit surprising, as I thought about it, that they were comfortable and accepting of me offering the ceremony. I looked up again at the fire. This time the flames appeared to be alive, like happy fire people holding hands and dancing in a circle. This perspective brought me much joy. I felt that I was completing the ceremony correctly and that Pachamama accepted the offering. After the fire had finished burning, my mother accompanied me as I checked the ashes. The ashes were a beautiful white color with just a touch of blue.

Just then Antonio awoke, asking, "What is happening?" I told him all that had happened. He went over to read the ashes. By now, all of my friends and family came outside to see what was happening. Antonio said, "This is very good. The Mother Earth did accept the offering and was very pleased with your ceremony." Then everyone hugged saying, "Que sea buena hora!" (This is a wonderful moment.) We all expected many blessings to follow.

When everyone left, I told Antonio what I saw in the fire. He told me that everything happens as it is meant to happen. "Pacha knows," he said. Antonio then hugged me and welcomed me as a brother on the path of the Pacha, the Cosmos, the Divine.

I realized that I had performed my first ceremony and was accepted by my community as a chacaruna. My scientific perspective was always still with me, but I now came to realize that the spiritual path was becoming my passion. The new business and my beautiful family would keep me grounded in the modern world, but my heart longed for the ageless, spiritual teachings of the Incas. I had to admit to myself that, however reluctantly, I was increasingly embedded in the spiritual path.

# ELDERS FROM THE MOUNTAINS

The Q'ero community is considered by some anthropologists to be very close to the pure language and customs of the ancient Inca people, with little outside contamination. The Q'ero have lived on Ausangate Mountain at an altitude of 14,000 feet for untold centuries. They are widely respected for their unique textiles, their healing powers, and their connection to the Apukunas and Mother Earth. The Ausangate Mountains are in the Cusco Region of Peru. It is a three-day journey by truck or horse, and much longer on foot, from Cusco to the five Q'ero communities. When I started my work as a tour guide, I heard that the Q'eros had remained pure Inca, without colonial or modern influences. It was said that they presently live much the same as the people in the mountains had lived centuries ago. Even today, you may only visit their remote communities with a special invitation.

# Cusi Pata

Happy Terrace is the name of a small square near the main square of the city of Cusco. The Wakay Pata, or main-square of this former capital of the Inca Territory, has an important shrine that connects the city to the Mother Earth. In the Andean tradition, August is the month when the Mother Earth opens her arms to receive the gifts of her children. Some people say that this is because the month of August is hot and the Mother is hungry. It was very windy one August afternoon that I walked from the main square a few meters to Cusi Pata, the Happy Terrace. As a collector of textiles, my eye was drawn to the clothing worn by two men and one woman standing in one corner of the small plaza. I immediately recognized the textiles as being Q'ero. I walked toward them to possibly meet some Q'ero people. As I approached, they noticed me and asked, "Do you want a despacho?" Despachos are sometimes pre-assembled and sold in the plaza during the time of special ceremonies. I replied that I was not looking for a despacho but that I would like to talk with them. We stood near a doorway and continued the conversation in Quechua, their native tongue. I wanted to learn the Q'ero point of view of the Inca traditions, beliefs, and ceremonies. Every community within the Andean world has a unique outlook on everything and slightly different beliefs. Nothing is considered absolute for the Incas except the One God, the Pacha, the Cosmos.

I was quite excited to meet the Q'ero. I wanted to know if I could visit their community and spend some time with them. One of the Q'ero men said that it was possible and that they would welcome my visit. However, they had come to Cusco to perform ceremonies and blessings throughout the month. I understood this since the first days of August are the most significant for special offerings, but the ceremonies extended well into the month. In some Andean communities, the people believe that the first days of August reveal the weather for the coming year. For example, the weather on August first would predict the weather for the upcoming January. Likewise, the weather on August second would foretell the climate for the month of February. In this fashion, they would predict how the weather would affect the anticipated crops. It was very important in the pre-Incan times to predict the weather so one could pray for the growth of the crops. Agriculture was the basis of the economy. So, during the early days of August, many offerings were made to Mother Earth to insure a prosperous year. This tradition is still carried on in slightly altered forms in farming communities and larger cities, such as Cusco and Puno.

A gentleman came over to the group and asked the Q'ero to do a ceremony for him. Knowing that they needed to leave, I said that I was happy to have met them and perhaps we would meet again. As the Q'ero departed, they smiled and said in unison, "*Tupananchiscama*," meaning, "Until I encounter you again." In the Andes, we do not say goodbye. We say until I encounter you again, which could be in any reality. In many of our expressions, there is a mixing of the physical and metaphysical meanings. In the Andean tradition, we do not separate the physical from the metaphysical.

# Mariano

After this first meeting with the Q'ero, I always tried to find other Q'ero people to meet with some of the people on my tours. Now that I knew that Q'ero were living in the Cusco area during the month of August, I asked some of my friends to be on the lookout and introduce me to other Q'ero people. I let it be known that I would like to employ their services in Cusco. Later in the month, Mariano came to me as a substitute for another Q'ero paq'o, who was to do a ceremony for a small tour group from the United States. Mariano called himself an Alto Misayoc (Quechua name for High Priest). As a High Priest in his community, Mariano was recognized to have all the powers at his disposal. He could call the Apus. He could work with the Universal Energy. He could do healings. He could perform any ceremony. He could interact with the Three Worlds. The physical features of the Q'ero are distinguishable from other indigenous people. Mariano is a man of average build and soft facial features. His skin color is quite light in shading, and his eyes are small and gentle. It is rare to see him not smiling. I found him to be charismatic, as well as very happy. These are known characteristics of the Andean Priests and Priestesses. I felt fortunate to have met Mariano and to have him lead us in one of their traditional Q'ero ceremonies.

# The Bumpy Road

t was some months later when I was able to take a few days from my work and accept an invitation from Mariano to visit his home. It was a little before dawn when I found the truck that was heading to Ausangate Mountain. Cusco was already coming alive with the street vendors collecting the vegetables from the trucks arriving from the mountain. Vendors were arriving with their products to set up their displays at their designated market stations. Everywhere in the area you could see people greeting each other and joyfully starting their day. Corner shops that served breakfast to the vendors were opening their doors as many people stopped in to buy their morning meal. I told the truck driver that I was going to Ausangate. I quickly purchased coca tea and small wheat bread for myself and as a gift for the Q'ero. You can only get this particular type of bread in Cusco, and I always enjoy it. The bread is made from stone ground flour that is ground fresh each day in Cusco.

The sun was ready to rise with the first light when I boarded the truck with my breakfast and my bag of gifts. The truck only goes to Ausangate on Tuesdays and Saturdays, so there were about twenty people already in the back of the truck when I climbed aboard. Everyone was sitting on bags of goods that were being transported to the mountains. I found a fairly comfortable spot to sit on the left side of the truck. In a few moments, the driver collected the equivalent of a couple of dollars from each person and closed the gates of the back of the truck. The top of the truck was left exposed since it was clear and no rain was expected.

The first hour and a half after we left Cusco the trip was comfortable.

Conversation was sparse since it was still early, and many people used this time to nap after rising so early to board the truck. The next couple of hours were very different as the truck turned off the paved roads and started to climb up the mountains. To say that the road was bumpy was to describe it at its best. Since it was a dirt road, there were many gullies and ruts caused by the trucks during the rainy season. All the passengers on the truck had to hang on to something fixed to avoid being thrown about. The road was only wide enough for one vehicle to pass. If another vehicle came from the opposite direction, one of the vehicles had to back up to a spot that was a little wider, allowing them to pass one another. This maneuvering was rather tricky because the mountain roads have sheer drops, no guardrails for protection, and many twists and turns. Fortunately, we only met one other truck on our journey. At one spot the truck had to drive through a stream about a foot and a half deep and 20 yards wide, just shallow enough to cross safely.

The truck had to stop twice during the daylong trip. One time there was a problem with one of the tires. The other time the engine was starting to overheat and the driver needed to put water in the radiator. As we went up the mountain the scenery changed. At lower levels, the landscape was green with many terraces, bordered by stones and filled with crops. These terraces, rising up the mountainside like giant steps, were constructed in pre-Incan times to stop the erosion of the soil on the mountain slopes. The terraces are still in use today for the same purpose. Terraces were called *pata-pata*. From this Quechua word, the Spanish named the most abundant crop that grew on these terraces high in the mountains patata(s) or papa(s). This is the source of the word potato. As the truck climbed upward, the green was disappearing and I started to see the strong grass called ichu. Rugs are woven with this grass. More importantly, ichu is a food source for the South American cameloids, such as llama, alpaca, huanaco, and vicuna. I saw mainly alpaca and llama grazing on the hillsides that day.

When I arrived at the truck's final stop, Mariano's cousin Jose met me for the long journey to Mariano's village. Jose was expecting me to stay with him and his family for the night. We had an evening meal and then Jose offered me some blankets made of alpaca wool for my bedding. I spent a comfortable night and slept until dawn. We enjoyed a breakfast of boiled meat, potatoes, corn, and fava beans. We ate our fill and put the remaining food in a piece of white cloth with Q'ero designs woven on the borders. We walked to the back garden where the animals were kept at night and mounted horses to continue the journey. We progressed slowly up the hill to the small community of Q'ochamoco, where we stayed the night in a rustic house. The wind whistled through this adobe house throughout the night. We slept again on alpaca throws or blankets on the dirt floor. It was uncomfortable, but adequate shelter for the night.

We set out early in the morning for Mariano's village, eating what food we had left. The road was very steep and made many sharp turns as we wound our way up the mountain. The horses were sure footed and knew the way. At times the horses would slip on the loose stones. You could hear rocks tumbling over and over as they sought a resting place hundreds of feet below. This slippage could be worrisome as there were sheer drops of many hundred feet at the side of the narrow trails. The horse I was riding seemed quite confident even if I wasn't. We arrived at the village before noon. Mariano and his family were there to welcome us with smiling faces. They knew, of course, that we were arriving. They said that the family dog also knew we would be coming that day, because all morning the dog was wagging his tail and jumping from place to place in anticipation. We all laughed and my memorable visit began. I laughed many times in the next few days with these somewhat mysterious and charming people.

# The Village

In Mariano's village, about thirty houses made of stones and adobe were spread over an area of about a square mile. The houses had thatched roofs and the kitchens were separate little rooms that were attached to or next to the main house. Some of the kitchens had an oven, but not all. Every household had an area next to the house that was surrounded by a low stone enclosure for the animals. In fact, most houses had a number of these areas for various livestock. The houses in the village were joined together by dirt paths, not roads. Some houses were quite high on the side of the mountain. There were several wells from which to draw water, but there was no plumbing and no electricity. Most of the people in the village were related to one another as a large extended family. All of the children addressed adults as tio or tia (uncle or aunt). Therefore, I was Tio Jorge Luis. This custom is usual in the Andes, so I was quite comfortable being Tio Jorge Luis.

Many of the children and a few adults were curious about me, so I went about greeting the people in the village upon my arrival. The Q'ero speak Quechua, but they speak a very old, maybe even the original, Quechua dialect. I did not have any difficulty communicating with them in Quechua, but they had many words for the spiritual aspects of the Inca traditions that were new to me.

The community was very similar in physical aspects to Paratia. However, in this sector of the Q'ero community, there was no center square as there was in Paratia. Both had open markets, held one day of each week. Immediately I saw their clothing was unique. The Q'eros' ponchos are much longer than those of any other community. Up until the 1940's, the Andean world only used natural dyes for their fabrics. After this time, they used many synthetic dyes which were much brighter in color. Although they do have some brightly hued ponchos, the Q'ero usually use natural or more subdued colors for their everyday ponchos. Their hats are always colorful with long tassels and beads in all the colors of the rainbow. In all of the Andes, you can identify each man's community by the colors and designs in his knitted woolen hat. You can also distinguish if he is married or single and what position he holds in the community by his hat. At fiesta time, in the large native outdoor markets, each man offers an observer a great deal of information solely by the hat he is wearing.

# Trial Marriage

Mariano was married, as are most Q'ero men. He and his wife had five children. A few days before my arrival, Mariano's nephew, Ricardo, was just finishing a trial marriage and the families were preparing for the wedding ceremony. The celebration of the marriage lasts three days or more. In most of the Andean highlands (above 14,000 feet), the couple would have a trial marriage for one to three years before the final commitment for life. After the final commitment, over ninety percent of the couples remain together. The courtship begins at the annual pilgrimage at Q'oyllorritti, when the teenagers from the seven Q'ero communities have the opportunity to meet and slip off for their romantic trysts. If the young man is interested in continuing the relationship, he takes a small mirror and reflects the sunlight to the girl as she tends the animal in the fields. Often, this is done from one mountainside to another.

If the affections continue and become serious, the couple enters into a trial marriage by living together in the young man's community. If the relationship becomes quarrelsome and falls significantly out of harmony, the elders in the community confront the couple, usually suggesting that they separate. If the couple births a baby during the trial marriage, the maternal grandparents raise the child as their own. The daughter would be free to seek another union, as would the young man she was living with. This custom has been successful and commonplace in all the highlands for many centuries. Even though the Catholic Church has always forbidden this long-standing tradition, it has survived and is still practiced in the highlands.

Marriage and family are strong bonds in all the communities of the highlands. Rarely do people divorce after the period of trial marriage. There is much closeness in spirit as well as proximity. In most houses the entire family shares one bedroom. Sometimes, when there are many children, the family has two bedrooms. Sexual relations are considered natural but discreet. Mariano and his wife, Serena, were typical of Q'ero couples. They shared a great deal of affection and respect. They were relaxed with each other and readily laughed together. The marital roles are quite defined, with both men and women working very hard. The men are responsible for and manage the agricultural realm of the community. An important tool used by the men, a *taquijaclla*, looks like a long stick with a cross member fifteen inches from the end. When the point of the stick is placed into the ground, the man's foot can step on and push the stick deep into the soil. As the taquijaclla is moved forward and backward, the hardened ground is loosened for planting.

The women labor physically as well as tend the animals in the fields while knitting, often with a baby strapped to their backs. Women are respected in the Q'ero community, especially for their intuitive powers. Officially, men have the final say, both in the family and in the community. However, the women control the money. So everyone has their own role and influence. Everyone in the community enjoys a good joke and many of their jokes point out the natural characteristics of a person or of his or her behavior. For example, if someone is very tall and thin, they would have a special descriptive nickname for that person that everyone, even the tall person, would accept. During my visit, the Q'ero seemed to find delight and laughter in much of their everyday life together.

The people in the community were very busy preparing for the wedding celebration, scheduled for the following week. Mariano had to arrange some of the details of the celebration in the morning, but was able to share time with me in the afternoon. After the noon meal, we walked further up the mountain to a spot that had a spectacular view of other mountains, not far in the distance. You could feel the presence of the mountains' energy and beauty. We were in the close company of many Apus.

# Apukunas

For the Andean people, the most important representatives of the Spirits or Light Beings are the Apukunas. Apukunas or Apus, are the Spirits that live on the mountains, and the people here "talk" with them on a daily basis. The Apus are part of the Upper World, but are linked to humanity in this Middle World of experience. All of the Andean communities, regardless of their language use the word and concept of "*chakra*." The translation of the word is "a field," but it refers to a field that has a crop growing in it. For the people, their chakra includes the fields, the animals, the house, and the family. The Apu's chakra includes the minerals, the crops, the animals, and the people under the protection of the Apu on their particular mountain. However, an Apu can assist and work with any person, near or far, who makes contact with that particular Apu and asks for the Apu's assistance or intervention in the Upper World.

Some people visualize the Apu, the Spirit of the Mountain, with the body of a human being with wings and the head of a Condor. Some people in the city hold meetings in closed rooms where a group of people meditates with someone identified as a paq'o who calls forth the Apu. There is then the sound of wings beating and a rush of air in the room, and people hear the voice of the Apu. I have never experienced such a thing, and Mariano said that he has never heard of this happening in the highland. I respected Mariano's opinion, as he was known in many communities for his ability to communicate with the Apus.

Mariano could read people and know who was in harmony with the Apus. This ability was considered a sign that these people could develop healing powers or the knowledge of how to communicate in the different Worlds. After we talked a bit about the beauty of the mountains, Mariano said, "Jorge Luis, I am honored that you came to visit with me. The Apus have told me that you are in strong harmony with them." This was very good news for me, since the Apus, like people, respond to those who also recognize and honor them. I was pleased to be seen in this way.

Mariano continued to talk about the Apus. "The Apus are like ancestors. These wise and loving grandfathers care for us and want to teach us about the Cosmos. It is possible that special agreements can be made with a particular Apu, and the Apu would grant you special powers." Mariano looked directly at me when he added, "But pay close attention to the Apu, for there often is a 'catch' or condition for having and retaining these powers. A person may be asked to do healings every week in the community and not accept reimbursement for their endeavors. Another may be sent to other communities or cities to teach others the unique sway of this particular Apu." Mariano seemed to be looking far into the mountains as he continued. "A few are 'initiated' by the Apus. They are asked to make a pilgrimage into the Snow Mountains with no clothing. It is a test to see if they are brave enough to trust the particular Apu to protect them from getting ill or dying from the elements." I asked Mariano if he had been initiated. His only reply was a smile. In a few moments he added, "Tonight, we will have a ceremony and call the Apus."

Some people believe that there are only male Apus. Others believe that there are also female Apus. A paq'o or yatiri will hear a very strong or stern voice from a specific Apu. Other Apus will have softer and calmer voices. There is even a tradition about Apu families who communicate with each other. Once again, each community carried on the oral traditions of the Apus in slightly different ways. All are considered to be correct in the Andean World. Only the Cosmos is seen as absolute. Everything else is subject to the community's experiences and beliefs.

Mariano pointed to the sky and said, "Look the Apus are talking. We can see their messages in the clouds." Seeing that many clouds had gathered and were moving rapidly in the wind, Mariano laughed and said, "Our despacho is being discussed among many Apus. The ceremony tonight might be very crowded." He suggested that the ceremony have the intention of my being able to communicate directly with the Apus. I agreed and found my heart beating just a little faster in anticipation of what might unfold.

# "Take It Away"

The ceremony proposed by Mariano was to take place at a special site, high on the mountain, at sunset. Since it was late November, the sun was setting in the mountains around six o'clock in the evening. Mariano, Pasqual, Teodor, Serena, and I started our walk up the mountain about 5:15 in the afternoon to prepare the mesa, or altar, for my special ceremony. I could hardly contain my excitement. I had participated in many ceremonies with Mariano as High Priest. I found him to be very powerful in his concentration and intent. It was an honor for him to offer to hold a special ceremony centered on my spiritual development.

We encountered *apachetas* as we walked up the path to a knoll that was near the top of the mountain. At any apacheta, you will find a pile of stones. Many of them are quite small and have been carried here from far away places. Each stone represents a sorrow, a feeling of guilt, known and unknown fears, or any other heavy energy that people want to leave behind. The translation of apacheta is "Take it away!" The people on their way to the shrine, usually on top of the mountain, are preparing their minds and hearts for the offering or ceremony at the shrine. They say a prayer to Mother Earth and place each stone with its intention on the pile. It is common, as you are walking in the highland, to see apachetas along the path climbing ever upward to a pre-Incan or Incan Shrine.

# Preparing the Mesa

After placing stones at two apachetas, we arrived at the offering place at about 5:30 in the late afternoon. We had a half hour before sunset to prepare the mesa. Great care is taken in preparing the mesa or altar. Everything has a ritualistic meaning and each element needs to represent the very best of its kind to honor the Apus or Pachamama. You only offer the best of what you have. The first item of the mesa is the cloth or piece of textile that is hand woven for this special purpose. The Q'ero are known throughout the highlands for the intricacies and quality of their mesa textiles. The fabric to be used in this ceremony had been made by Serena. Being a collector of textiles, I was particularly interested in the mesa cloth she created.

The colors of the background of this cloth were mainly brown and black. The mesa or altar cloths always have two panels, one male and one female, joined together with one thread woven from top to bottom. Lloque is the left side and *pana* is the right. The shades of color of the two sides looked different. Serena explained that the color of the wool is the same on both sides, but one side is woven in the opposite direction of the other, giving the appearance of difference when they were really the same. She added, "Men and women may appear different in this world, but at the energetic level they are the same." Different symbols were woven into the cloth in brighter colors. The design always contains symbols of the sun, the Sacred Lake, offerings, crops, flowers, etc. They are carefully woven into the cloth to reflect the perspective of the particular family who made the textile. The women usually spin the wool and weave the fabric in their unique designs. These cloths are a matter of great reverence and pride. I particularly liked the design and workmanship of this cloth and hoped that Serena would consider selling it to me following the ceremony.

Many items were reverently placed on the cloth. In the highlands, the participants will first place coca leaves on the mesa. Then they will unwrap many little packages of special ingredients and place them beside the mesa cloth for use in the ceremony. Mariano had carried these packages in his ceremonial bag. In the cities, the offering or despacho can be purchased already assembled. Here, high on Ausangate Mountain, Mariano had assembled the ingredients, according to his own style and preferences. After the coca leaves, Mariano next arranged his ancient power stones, *cuyas*, that he received from his teacher. Wine and chicha were poured into shells, which were then placed in two corners of the mesa. The shells represent Mama Cocha, the spirit of the sea and the lake. Mama Cocha is considered one of the most important aspects of the Divine Mother in the care of the people in this vicinity of the Sacred Lake. Between the seashells, Mariano placed a cross made of a special wood from the jungle, called *chonta*. Chonta is a very dark hardwood that comes from a type of palm that grows in many regions of the jungle. It is considered a sacred wood and is used in ceremonial crosses, as well as other Incan Power Tools. Next to be placed on the Mesa was a *conopa*, a ceramic piece in the form of a sitting llama. There is a hole in the center of the conopa that Mariano filled with llama fat, a necessary ingredient in the offering. This particular conopa had been handed down for many, many generations in the Q'ero community. Some conopas are made of crystal, granite, or various kinds of stones. This one was made of marble and had an iridescent look coming from the many years of service. After this special ceremony, I began to collect conopas, and I now often give them as gifts after their use in a special ceremony.

# Calling the Apus

ariano reached into his bag that held his coca leaves. I was intrigued with this ceremonial coca bag. I had never seen anything like it before. Everyone in the highlands has a bag for their coca leaves that is made of textiles in their community design, but this bag was different. It had gray feathers with a few black feathers in contrast. I asked Mariano, when I first saw the bag, what it was made of. He told me that it was made from the skin, with the feathers still attached and growing, from the neck of a condor. It was very soft and beautiful and also had great ceremonial meaning since the condor was the messenger to the Apus. Mariano took coca leaves from this bag, blew his messages on them, and released them into the wind to travel to the Apus. In a loud voice, Mariano called to the Apus as he released the coca leaves. "Apu Ausangate – Apu Salcantay – Apu Wakac Willka – Apu Pachatusan – Apu Machu Picchu - Apu Wayna Picchu – Apu Putu Cusi – Mama Simona Apu." Serena then called to all of the Pachamamas in a similar manner. Suddenly, the wind made its presence known by gently brushing across everyone's faces. Facing the wind, Mariano turned to his left and, in a sweeping motion, rotated to the right while slowly calling the wind's name, UUWWWW AAAAAAA AAAAAA AAYYYYYY YYYYYYYYRR RRAAAA AAAAAAAA *Waira.* Silent calm came to the mesa. Mariano then greeted each person and asked permission to do the ceremony. He also greeted Pachamama and asked the Mother's permission. We then started to chew the coca leaves, always choosing the best leaves available. Mariano said, "They taste good. We can begin." Mariano and his assistant, along with Serena and her assistant, began to choose the best leaves and arrange them with intention on the mesa. Mariano placed three coca leaves in a pile for each Apu, while Serena placed two coca leaves for each of the Pachamamas.

# Words of Preparation

A few moments before the ceremony was to begin, Mariano pulled me aside. We walked a short distance from the place where the materials for the despacho were being prepared. Mariano looked at me with a serious yet soft expression on his face. "My friend," he said, "I feel in my heart that this ceremony will be very important to you. Before we begin, I want to offer you the seeds of knowledge of the true Inca Laws that have been handed down in our community from the very early times. The Inca Laws that will help you open your heart to the messages of the Apus are Munay, Llancay, and Yachay. The meanings are important to understand not only with your mind but also with your heart. *Munay* means love for everything that is surrounding us. *Llancay* means work or service as a blessing in your individual expression of this reality. *Yachay* means the opening of your heart to the understanding of the Cosmos, in other words, wisdom. I will pray that your heart accepts the seeds of these Laws today and that their meaning grows as you meditate on their meaning in your life." These words resonated in my heart as we walked back to join the others.

# The Ceremony

Mariano started to pray with his eyes closed so that he could listen with his heart and hear the words that flowed through it. Mariano asked for forgiveness for all of us in order to rid us from any spiritual hindrances that were blocking our hearts. He spread a white paper on the mesa. On the paper, Mariano carefully arranged alternating red and white carnation petals shaped in a semi-circle. He then dipped one red carnation flower into the wine and shook droplets of wine over the paper in a blessing. He repeated this ritual with the chicha. Mariano next placed a rectangle of cotton below the petals and placed a shell in the center of the cotton. He stood up and proceeded to bless the four corners of the grounds where the ceremony was being conducted with incense in the sign of the cross. Mariano returned to the Mesa, sprinkled the paper with a dusting of colorful confetti, introduced pieces of wool, the colors of the rainbow, and spread gold and silver papers opened like two flags. Everything was sprinkled with colored sugar. Other ingredients placed in the center in artistic form were candies, dehydrated potatoes, rice, corn, coca seeds, and beans. Small metal objects representing everyday life were caringly arranged throughout the despacho.

Everyone took a turn adding each ingredient employing his or her own unique design. Candles and candies, in the symbolic forms of animals, houses, etc. were placed in pairs on the rim of the white paper. Special prayers were spoken by Mariano to help us rid ourselves of the heavy energies as he sprinkled confetti over the entire design. Again, everyone took part, and the offering now had become a work of art involving all the participants. It was very colorful and rich in design. At this point, Mariano added several glass balls, crystallized from sand struck by lightening. Pasqual handed Mariano a llama fetus wrapped, or dressed, in cotton and colorful wool strands. Mariano gently placed it on top of the offering. In the Andean world, the llama is the symbol of love and service. This ritual llama fetus is charged with carrying the intentions or messages into another reality, the Spirit World of the Apus

Mariano then took a kintui of three coca leaves and placed them in the design of a flower on the white paper while intoning an intention. He asked for a blessing for all present, for the community, for the crops, for the animals, and for all special intentions. Each intention, prayer, or request was placed in a separate kintui. Each person then participated in a similar fashion. A small piece of llama fat was then placed on top of each kintui pile. Mariano ended the intonation by asking that the Apus allow me to connect directly with them from my heart.

After I placed my last kintui on the offering, I turned around to walk back to the place where I had been standing. As I fully stood up, I looked into the distance at the mountains as the sun was setting. I was looking into another reality. The mountains had all merged into one mountain. This mountain that filled the horizon, was dark, almost black. I could see the aura of the mountain. Light, in the colors of blue, white, and pink, seemed to emanate from the mountain like a band of flames burning from untold candles. At that moment, I experienced the connection of the Apus and the chacaruna. I was having a transcendental experience of the connecting Worlds without the use of sacred plants or hallucinogenics. I was unaware of space and time.

Only when Pasqual asked if I wanted to offer additional intentions with coca leaves did I return to this reality. I felt disoriented for a few seconds, but then I smiled and said my request had already been answered. The joy in my heart must have been reflected in my face as everyone embraced me.

I looked at the mountains and the last remnants of light from the sunset. The scene was beautiful, but it could not compare to the moment when I saw them with my heart. My consciousness seemed to have burst open into a new level of connectedness with the Divine and all there is. There are not adequate human words to describe the sense of oneness I experienced.

Now that the offering was complete, Mariano carefully folded the paper filled with the ingredients into a bundle that he secured with woolen threads and tied in a bow. He first placed it on his heart and then on top of Serena's head, requesting that Pachamama absorb all remaining heavy energies. He proceeded to perform this ritual with each participant. Next, Mariano handed Serena the offering. She embraced the package and pressed it to her heart, her forehead, and over her head, requesting the acceptance of everyone's intentions. We all followed and prayed for all of the intentions, ours and those of the other participants.

Pasqual prepared a place to burn the offering a few yards away, as Mariano led the procession to this spot. Mariano placed the offering on a bed of wood gathered earlier in the day. The offering was set afire. As I watched the flames, I reflected on my experience a few moments earlier. My heart vibrated with a knowledge that is not bound by the intellectual mind. A sense of bliss awakened from deep within me. I both wanted to secretly nurture this inner experience and, at the same time, share it with others so that they might join me in the bliss. I now stood solidly on the path of the chacaruna from which I could not, would not, turn.

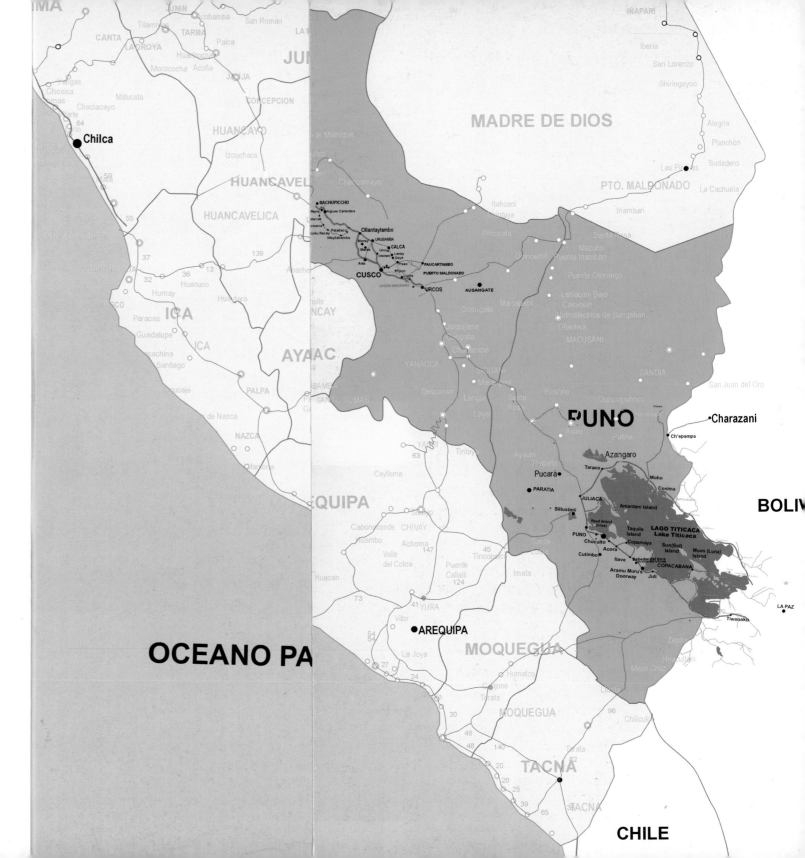

**TOP (L–R)**
Hitching Post of the Sun, Machu Picchu
View of Moray
Condor head, Condor Temple, Machu Picchu
Steps and temples at Ollantaytambo
**BOTTOM**
Water channels at Tipon

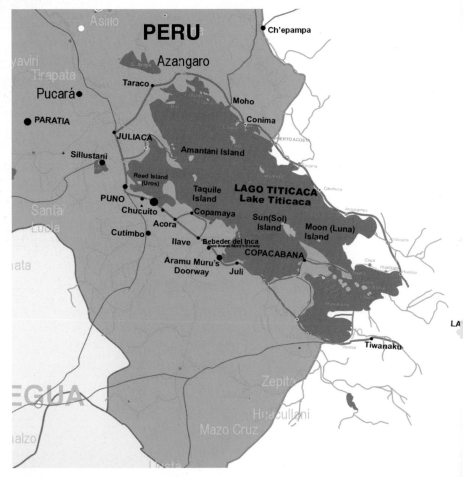

**TOP (L–R)**
View of Lake Titicaca
View of Sillustani
**BOTTOM (L–R)**
Reed boat and close-up of Uros Island
Reed boat and Uros Island on Lake Titicaca

**TOP (L–R)**
Aramu Muru's Doorway full view
Jorge Luis standing in one channel
Aramu Muru's Doorway with one energy channel
**BOTTOM (L–R)**
Aramu Muru's Doorway close up
Jorge Luis standing in Aramu Muru's Doorway

**TOP (L–R)**
Paratia Dancers
Paratia Paq'os
**BOTTOM (L–R)**
People of Taquile
Paratia Dancer

TOP (L–R)
A young mountain cara cara
Mountains of th High Palteau in Peru
BOTTOM (L–R)
Chullpas at Cutimbo
An offering or despacho to Pachamama

**ABOVE**
Mariana, Qu'ero Yatari, performing an offering to Pachamama
**OPPOSITE**
**(TOP)** Twelve Shell despacho to Charazani
**(BOTTOM)** Dehydrated potatoes, quinoa, and cheese
**(INSET)** Snake, Puma, and Condor, representing the Three Worlds

(TOP) Jorge Luis Delgado and his mother, Margarita
(BOTTOM) Kotunas, National Flower of Peru

# HIGH PLATEAU

lat, majestic, and desolate, the formidable mesas of the landscape Temple of the High Plateau seem to erupt from the valleys of the Andes around Lake Titicaca. The High Plateau is the biggest natural altar on the planet Earth, surrounded by two Coldierra, Oriental and Occidental. It is called "House of God or Divinity." This region is called *Raya*, which also means line, referring to the ley line or earth energy line. Raya is the *abra*, or doorway to the High Plateau. From Raya, one river travels to the Sacred Valley and another river flows to the Sacred Lake. The vast High Plateau covers an area of 50,000 square miles. It lies between Peru and Bolivia and surrounds Lake Titicaca, the Sacred Lake. In the Inca tradition, this lake is the origin of the culture. In Incan times, it was called the Colla Suyo, meaning "the nation of the medicine." The High Plateau is fulcrum of the coast, jungle, and Snow Mountains. It is also my home.

Lake Titicaca has always played an important role in the agriculture of this region because it warms the temperature by five degrees and makes the climate more conducive to growing varying crops. From ancient times, the people created technology to increase the production of the crops. They invented the pata patas, waru waru, cochas, and conchas. The pata patas were terraces formed of earth and bordered by stones that stopped erosion of soil on the steep mountains and allowed the people to plant crops successfully. The most important crop in the pata patas was potato. The waru waru are the channels that the people dug in rows around and between the crops. They filled the channels with water that stored the warmth of the sun and prevented the crops from freezing in the cold nights. The algae that grew in the bottom of the channels was a natural fertilizer for the land. The cochas are artificial lakes that the people created to change the temperature. The conchas are the stone walls that were built around the fields to keep the crops warm and to protect the crops from the wind and grazing animals.

Unlike the surrounding mountain peaks, some landscape altars of the Pre-Inca and Inca people seem to have had their peaks sheared off to form these immense plateaus for mysterious and otherworldly purposes. On many of these mesas or altars you will find chullpas, usually thought of as burial towers. However, many paqo's and yatiris tell of traditions that used them for ceremonial purposes. Since our Pre-Inca and Inca ancestors did not think of the physical and metaphysical as really being different realities, it is probable that the chullpas had various uses. They stand in different states of decomposition as monuments to civilizations that came to this Power Place or Sacred Site for untold eons. Further to the Southwest near Lake Titicaca is another less visited site with both round and rectangular chullpas. This landscape altar rises nearly two and a half miles above sea level and is located in the vicinity of Moon Valley.

# Cutimbo

The air was pristine and the sun cast many shadows on the afternoon when I arrived at Cutimbo with a small tour group of three people. You could see the two massive landscape altars rising from the valley in the distance as we drove from Puno into the Andes. Although not too many foreign tourists come to Cutimbo, this Sacred Site is well known to the local people. The government installed a small parking lot and prepared a pathway to the top of the mesa for visitors. We disembarked from the van and were walking towards the path when I noticed the first eagle soaring above. I immediately pointed to the majestic bird to call attention to it. Soon another eagle arrived and soared over our heads and through the valley. "This could be a very special day," I told the group. "It is not every day that eagles soar in this area at this time of the afternoon." We continued our climb with a little more excitement and anticipation. I love birds and have always studied their patterns.

A little more than halfway up the path, an area has been gated by the government. Here, in the side of the hill, is a prehistoric cave dwelling. The two people with me were very interested in this small cave and quickly noticed that there were ancient bones in one corner. There are also prehistoric drawings throughout the cave of people hunting, of South American cameloids, and of a design of a human body with bird feet and legs. In later times, this cave was used as a burial place, as is indicated by the remaining bones. Viewing the remnants of an ancient civilization gives us a physical connection to the ancestors and the inner world. We then continued up the path with thoughts of the ancestors foremost in our minds.

# Temples Amid the Crops

s we arrived at the top of the path, we gazed out into the valley and saw yet another flat mesa amid the climbing peaks of the other mountains. The top of Cutimbo is quite vast and perfectly flat, as far as the eye can see, except where two chullpas stand amid an area of about two square kilometers of stones and dirt. This place has only two entrances. It stands in the valley like a natural fortress of solid rock that defies intruders. As you walk in one area, you find a supposed burial ground with small stones placed in circles to indicate an underground tomb. Also dirt channels were used to irrigate crops in ancient times. The most predominate structure on this flat plain is a rectangular stone temple. This temple is constructed from precisely fitted large stones with some reddish sandstones crowning the top of the temples. The temple is about ten meters high but can only be entered by climbing on hand and knees like a puma through a small opening at ground level on the eastern wall of the temple.

Once inside, it takes a moment for your eyes to adjust to the low light. Then the interior reveals two floors to the temple. There are two large niches on each side that could each hold a human body. Many believe that these niches were meant to indicate the duality, the two aspects, male and female. When you stand inside, the left side feels feminine and the right feels masculine. On the west wall, there are three niches about chest high that are smaller and were perhaps used to hold power tools. These three niches represent the Three Worlds, the Pachas. Many carvings of snakes are on the exterior of the west wall.

We began our ceremony by chewing coca leaves and offering a local alcoholic drink to Pachamama to ask permission to conduct a special ceremony to release our heavy energies and emerge more in balance with our own masculine and feminine aspects. When we encounter our own energy, we have the balance and the strength of the puma, so we are ready to face our heavy energies, *hucha*. First, we formed a kintui of coca leaves and blew our feminine aspects into the leaves. We then placed them in the masculine niche on the right. We repeated the ceremony in the opposite form for our masculine aspects.

Having balanced our energies, we sat and meditated on what heavy energies, sorrows, regrets, etc., we were carrying in our hearts. We then stood and offered a kintui, holding our heavy energies, to each niche of the Three

Worlds. In the second part of the ceremony, we called the Apukunas, the Light Beings, and again offered the kintui with the intention of increasing our refined energy, *sami*. We also placed our wishes for ourselves and those dear to us in this offering. At the end of the ceremony, we crawled out of this comfortable temple with a feeling of lightness, joy and hope. We emerged into the east, the direction of the sunrise.

# Transcendental Pumas

As we came out into the sunlight, we paused only for a moment before we walked over and stood next to the rectangular temple, with it to our right side, the masculine side. On our left stood a round chullpa, which is just a little bit smaller than its mate. Both chullpas had a small band of stone around the entire structure, like a headband. The round chullpa represents the feminine aspect and correctly stood to our left. Again, we were able to balance our own energies amid these ancient temples. Now the round one is closed, but I have been inside this chullpa in earlier times. Round seats with a niche on top of each seat surround the circular structure and face the door. It is a comfortable space. Certainly this temple was used for gatherings, other than solely as a burial place. Possibly these temples were used as places for initiations. Initiates would have to face their fear of physical death to understand and participate in the pursuit of their spiritual paths. Here, in the presence of the ancestors, the initiates would receive their support and blessings.

Protruding from the wall of the round temple are two puma heads and legs, carved convexly, as if embossed on the stone, appearing to emerge from the interior of the chullpa. The symbolic or transcendental meaning of this pair of pumas emerging from the chullpa is that by following the pathway of your power, and by balancing your own feminine and masculine energy, you can go through any obstacle, even physical walls. Next to the doorway are carvings of viscachas, small Andean animals, like a rabbit with a long tail. These are interesting animals because at sunrise they stand still in a prayer-like position. When they are in this praying position, the people will not hunt or kill them. A small round chullpa nearby also has a carving of one puma in its doorway. This puma looks like it is guarding the structure.

After briefly taking pictures, I took my friends away a few meters to an area where there were stones and dried grass. Hidden in the grass is a special stone. Carved into this stone of about a meter and a half is the likeness of a puma head with a lizard body and human hands. It seems like it is a process of metamorphosis. The lizard signifies the process of regeneration because if a lizard loses its tail, it can regenerate another. The lizard also represents the Underground World. The puma head, combined with the human hand, represent walking in this Middle World. This stone was probably part of another structure. For us today, it indicates that in the process of being human we pass through other stages. We will never know the original meaning intended by the carver, but it remains a wonderful mystery and a record of ancient beliefs. The most notable feature of this stone is its friendly energy. I would have liked to have known my ancestor who carved it. We would have had much to talk about.

# Mountain Cara Cara

Since I was a boy, I have been fascinated with the beauty of birds. From a young age, I could recognize various types of birds, even at a considerable distance. One of my favorite birds is the mountain cara cara. This majestic bird is neither an eagle nor a falcon. It looks as if it should belong to this family of birds, but it is distinct. Its feathers are black and white, and it has a distinctive bright red bill. When it flies, it spreads its tail feathers into a fan of alternating black and white feathers. Some people call this bird mariano, others call it chinalinda. Everyone considers it to be a symbol of good luck. I can remember when I was a young boy going to the market with my mother, riding on the back of a truck. For no apparent reason, the truck driver would stop the truck in the road. At first, I thought that there must be some mechanical problem, but this was not the reason. The truck driver stopped to leave the cab of the truck to go out and salute in a loud voice, "Good luck, mariano, good luck!" From that time, I have always looked into the distance when traveling, searching for this magnificent bird.

I first noticed the mountain cara cara this day when we emerged from the rectangular temple. It had flown very high from the west through the midday sun to the east. I followed the flight of the cara cara and noticed that as it flew across the sun, a halo surrounded the sun. I said, "Thank you, cara cara, for showing me this beauty." As soon as I had some free time from the official tour with my friends, I traveled alone to the other side of

Cutimbo. As I was walking, I noticed a large stone with white spots on top. I said to myself, "This stone reminds me of rocks that I saw eagles sitting on and sunning themselves on other trips." I decided to go there and sit on that rock. I had a beautiful view covering a great expanse. Feeling like the bird, a feeling of needing to fly came over me. Only by flying could I truly enjoy all the beauty. So, I was trying to jump; one, two, three times off the mountain. But my conscious mind was, fortunately, more cautious. I decided to meditate in order to do the flight in my mind. In this way, I could enjoy the sensation of flying.

Soon, my conscious mind called me back to the reality of the rock. However, on the return flight of my meditation, I noticed that over the edge of the cliff, an indentation of rock about three feet down held a nest of the cara cara. I was thrilled to have this extraordinary experience. I slid off the rock and moved over a few feet to physically view the nest. I leaned over the edge of the cliff and saw a nest of cara cara with two young birds. I flapped my arms as if to fly and communicated with them in my heart that I wanted to fly with them. The two birds left the nest and flew in a small circle close to the cliff, and then they flew in a larger circle. I watched in joy and amazement. On the flight of the third circle, one cara cara flew directly over my head and hovered only one meter above me. The sound of the wings was deafening. I experienced a confusion of feelings, including happiness, fear, and excitement. I was trying to understand what was wanted. It was a blessing, but my conscious mind ended the experience with many rational questions.

It was at this time that I understood that we really can speak many languages with the heart. We can speak to the birds. We can speak to the animals. We can speak to the rocks. We can speak to the crops, and we can speak to the Apus, the Light Beings. We can speak at least five languages with the heart. We can communicate with all of the five kingdoms (Mineral, Vegetable, Animal, Human, and Apukunas, or Light Beings). In the mineral kingdom, we have the two polarities of gold and silver, representing the male and female, respectively. For this reason, the Incas used gold and silver in their temple designs, representing all of the kingdoms, as part of the manifestation of creation. The gold represented the Father Sun and was used exclusively in the temples. Silver, representing the female energy of the moon, *Mama Killa*, was used in jewelry and ceremonial tools in conjunction with gold. Gold and silver were used for spiritual purposes and not for temporal value or as money.

In the vegetable kingdom, two important "daughters," Mama Sara and Mama Coca, represent corn and coca leaves. Mama Sara is the symbol of the physical food, and Mama Coca is the symbol of material food. Within the animal kingdom, we have the symbolic power animals of the Three Worlds: the Snake, the Puma and the Condor. In the human world, the Children of the Sun have the two aspects of male and female. The Upper World has the same aspects as the human world.

I returned into the moment and realized that I needed to rejoin my friends. Instantly, my scientific mind challenged my experience. "How was it possible to talk to birds? People will think that you are nuts." These thoughts rapidly flew through my conscious mind. My heart just quietly soothed me with a knowing connection to all the kingdoms, saying, "Be patient with your mind. It thinks that its thinking is all there is, but you have experienced that there are more ways to truly communicate than with the conscious mind that is only trained in the language of men." I was grateful for this realization of expanded languages, or ways of communication, with the many expressions of the Cosmos. I left this place with new spiritual tools and with great reluctance, as I felt so connected to all of creation during these joyous moments.

As I rejoined my friends, they were eager to tell me of their experiences around the chullpas. They saw many variations of color reflecting in the stones in the sunlight. We proceeded down the steep path to the car. We were on the road for about half an hour before I could relate to them my experience with the cara cara. They listened intently and were eager to know how to speak with the heart. I explained that this was a process of opening the heart through love and service. They laughed and said that they were grateful that my rational mind was ever present or I might have really jumped off the cliff and they would still be looking for me. We all laughed and decided that we had had a wonderful day at Cutimbo. Quietly, in my heart, I realized that I would forever view my surroundings differently, with a deeper connection to all creatures.

# Lupaka People

According to some anthropologists, the Lupaca people probably built Cutimbo. The term Lupaka comes from *lupi* and *haque*, meaning Children of the Sun. These people had their roots in the area around Lake Titicaca, from Puno to the border of Bolivia. The Lupaka believed that they were the Children of the Sun, and they worshipped the Father Sun, Inti Tata. They were aware that there was the Sun behind the Sun, Intij Inti. They named themselves the children of the Sun, Lupi Haque.

These people were prosperous. The discovery by the Spanish of these people in the Colonial Times was considered a gift to the Crown of Spain. The Spanish government sent an official to research the Lupakas as to the extent of their population and the reasons for their success. A census was conducted, their numbers recorded, and the secrets of the Lupakas were revealed. The Lupakas had their people seasonally working in the various ecological regions of the jungle, the coast, as well as in the High Plateau. They produced various diverse crops and products in the each region and brought the products back to the lake for their community's use and for trading with neighbors. The Lupaka used the region known as Moon Valley to raise the cameloids. The name Moon Valley is of more modern times. The valley was named because of the natural formations that look like a landscape of the moon.

Even in the time of the Incas, this valley was not conducive to growing crops. The Lupakas found that they could put the area to good use through the herding of animals, which thrived in this environment. In even more ancient times, interest in the unique stone formations led many people to construct small chullpas in this valley as tombs. Caves in the area revealed to the anthropologists many prehistoric drawings. It seems that the caves were used for habitation and to link with the Lower World. Perhaps, before going hunting, the native inhabitants made drawings to somehow manifest a successful hunt. The area around Cutimbo has been in active use in many ways for many centuries. Today, this area is still used to raise many animals, including cattle and sheep. It has always been the home of many large and majestic birds, like the eagle, falcon, and mountain cara cara, as well as home to our ancestors. The Lupaka people are now named Aymara, which, fortunately, is my heritage. It is then only natural that I have such a strong connection to Cutimbo and the Moon Valley.

# Amantani

ake Titicaca sits as a multifaceted shimmering blue jewel in the center of the natural landscape Temple of the High Plateau. In ancient times, the Lake was called the Eternal City. All of the islands on the Lake were considered to be temples. On each island you can find pre-Colonial buildings. Amantani is an island in the northern part of the Lake, approximately seventeen miles off the shores of Puno. It is a mountainous island and is approximately two and one half by three miles in size. It is home to eight villages and, to this day, has no form of transportation except by foot. Sitting high atop two peaks, facing the larger part of the Lake, are the Temple to the Father, Coanos in ancient language, and the Temple to the Mother, Pachamama.

The people of Amantani are mainly farmers, and the central crop is potatoes. Usually corn does not grow at this altitude, but on this beautiful island the people grow a special variety of corn. This corn traditionally had very small kernels and was solely used in ceremonies to Mama Sara in the Sacred Valley. Today, they still grow this corn, but it is now grown for food. In ancient times, the people from this island spoke Puquina. Today, they speak Quechua. Quarries are also on the island from which the people cut special building stones used to form the streets of Puno. The Amantani people today are known for their textiles and their hospitality. Each time I visit the island, a family warmly welcomes me into their home for food and a place to stay.

One of the most important festivals is held in late January. The people place flags in different colors of the potatoes (red, pink, purple, yellow, white, black, blue, or violet) around the top of the temples. They divide the people of the eight villages on Amantani into two sides. The people climb the Stone walkway and the numerous steps to the area of the Temples for the celebration. Upon reaching the top of the mountain and their respective Temple, the celebrants walk, circling their respective Temple in a direction that is counter to the spiral of the Cosmos. This action honors the belief that "as above, so below." The people believe that the present reality mirrors the movement of the Cosmos. One side represents the Temple of the Father, and the other side represents the Temple of Pachamama.

The two sides oppose each other in a lengthy footrace. If the side representing the Temple of Pachamama wins the race, there will be a year of plenty. Of course, there will be a lean year if the other side wins. Both sides race in earnest, even though they all hope for a plentiful crop. After the race there is a big fiesta in the flat area below the Temples. The people dance into the night. The main paq'o leads a ceremony of gratitude to the Mother Earth. They offer the essence (liquid) of the best of each of their crops to the Mother. They place the essence in an individual shell and toss the essence of the best back to the Mother Earth in gratitude. The festival reflects both the playful and industrious nature of the people of Amantani.

# Island Boat Ride

Traveling to the island is time-consuming. Until recently, the only way to get to the islands of Taquille or Amantani was on a wooden motorboat captained by natives from these islands. The trip from Puno takes about three hours, as these boats are not built for speed. Fortunately, we now have very fast boats that make the trip much shorter. The ride to Amantani takes you past the Reed Island of the Uros community. Since the boat ride seems endless, and I have taken it many times, it provides an opportunity for reflection without much interruption. It is easy to become mesmerized by the beautiful blue water with its dancing crystals of light reflecting the sunlight in rhythmic motion.

One reason that Amantani is so special or sacred is that the island sits directly on the ley line that connects Tiawanaku, Pukara, and Cusco. All these places are considered pre-Incan Sacred Sites. I was thinking about the ancient and mysterious nature of the island when we arrived at the small port on the northeast side of the island. I was pleased to arrive, as I had been looking forward to spending time with Maximo, a highly respected paq'o who lived on the island. I was met by my friend, Toribio, who offered to take some of my bundles for the short walk up the side of the mountain to his house. As we entered the courtyard, I again admired the precision and intricacy of the design that Toribio had made with the smooth small black and white stones. The black stones come from Amantani, and the white ones come from the island of Soto. These stones are used in many shrines, both in ancient times and currently. Today, these stones are being used to make shrines in the front of Catholic Churches in Peru that contain statues of the Madonna. Also, these stones are in Masonic Temples in various parts of the world.

Here, at Toribio's house, the stones formed the floor of the entire courtyard of twelve feet by eighteen feet. It was truly a work of art. I again told Toribio how much I enjoyed his work as I handed his wife, Sabina, a gift of fruit from the mainland. She accepted graciously and asked us to come to the table for the noontime meal. Since I was now hungry and knew that Sabina was an exceptional cook, I quickly put my things in the room prepared for me. Then I joined Toribio and his friend, Maximo, at the courtyard table. I was pleased to meet Maximo and we chatted about many things during the meal. Maximo was very respected on the island for his reading of coca leaves and his offering of ceremonies. During the conversation, Maximo told me about the sacred sites where he performs the ceremonies. I quickly asked him if he would take me to these special places only he knew about. At first, he seemed reluctant to do so. He spent some time talking to Toribio in private to see if Toribio thought I was sincere in my spiritual quest. Toribio convinced Maximo that I was very sincere and already walking the path. Maximo then offered to take me late in the afternoon to the Temples and other special sites on the island.

# Temples and Chincanas

Approximately half-way up the mountain path to the Temples, we left our stones on the apacheta stones placed there by previous climbers. We blew the intention of our heavy energies into the stones and left them for the Mother to transmute. Next, Maximo walked off the path about fifteen meters to a ledge on the side of the mountain, supporting a large rock formation. I did not understand why he had come here until I followed his example and hung the upper half of my body over the side of the smooth flat stone. I saw that, underneath, tucked into the stone was a natural crevice into which Maximo placed coca leaves and asked permission of Pachamama to proceed to the temple for the ceremony. This special crevice is hidden by nature. Maximo asked me to keep the location private and I, of course, agreed. We walked further up the path that leads to both Temples, offering coca leaves to Waira, the wind, and asking Waira to lead us to the proper Temple for the ceremony. Waira directed us to Coanos, Pacha Tata, and the Temple of the Father.

At the Temple of the Father, many terraces take the pyramid form. At the top of the tiers of terraces sits a square stone temple that has stood on this site since pre-Inca times. Like in Pukara and Tiawanaku, the Temple formation is both semi-subterranean and at ground level. It has at least three visible levels. In the subterranean level of the Temple, niches are carved in the stone both on the sides of the Temple and on the stone floor of the Temple. Maximo said that these holes or niches were places for different kinds of offerings. Around the perimeter on the ground level, mesas are used for the preparation of the kintui and other offerings. Maximo prepared the coca leaves, along with many symbols made of sugar, as an offering of gratitude to the Mother Earth and to the Father. We burned the offering and then placed the ashes in the niches in the lower level of the Temple. We offered prayers and set out for the other Temple, the Temple to Pachamama.

We arrived at Llacastiti, the Temple to Pachamama, shortly before sunset, the time that the paq'o deem best for the offerings to Mother Earth at this Sacred Site. This Temple is octagonal in shape and made of the same stone as the Father Temple. The floor is made of the earth and stones. In the middle of the Temple are five or six continuous concentric circles of earth edged with small stones. As I stood there in the smoke rising from the burning offering, I had the sensation of spinning in a spiral. I was standing with a kintui in each hand as I felt my energy merge with the energy of the Temple spiraling ever upward. We ended the ceremony again with prayer and began our descent down the mountain in the growing darkness. Before we parted, I asked Maximo if he would be willing to take me to the tunnel that I had heard existed on the island because he had retained a great deal of the oral traditions of the elders concerning access to this mysterious tunnel. He agreed and offered to take me to the spot early the next morning.

Toribio and I had just finished our breakfast when Maximo arrived. We invited him to have tea before we embarked on our mission. During the conversation, I related to Maximo my experience at Llacastiti, or Pachamama Temple. Maximo commented that this was a sign of a true communion with the Mother. We then left and walked to the place of the *chincana*, or tunnel. The main plaza of the island was about ninety yards from Toribio's house. We walked to the small church, or chapel, on the far side of the plaza and found an old house with a wooden door. Maximo said that the chincana was in this house. He pushed the door open, and we entered.

We were in an old house consisting of three windowless rooms. Two rooms seemed to be fifty or sixty years old and one from Colonial times. I noticed indentations where windows should be and crosses etched everywhere in the stone in different perspectives. I asked Maximo why there were so many crosses here. He started to laugh. Maximo said, "These crosses were made by the people who tried to live here, but strange energies forced them away. At one time, this place was also a police station, but there are no longer police on the island." I then asked, "Maximo where is the tunnel?" He said, "Under the ground." He then told me the history of the closing of the tunnel. Maximo again laughed as he said, "Once, the man who was hosting the local fiesta decided to close the tunnel. He didn't want to be responsible for some people who got drunk and might enter the tunnel and get lost there."

Then he pointed out the entrance to the tunnel in the floor of what once may have been a separate room in the older part of this house. I noticed some pre-Inca or Inca stone work on the main wall and on parts of two other walls. Perhaps an ancient room once surrounded the entrance. Maximo said that his grandmother told him that the tunnel was narrow for the first few yards and then widened. The legend was that this tunnel went all the way to Cusco and other Power Places on the same ley line. Maximo's grandmother said that people and animals would disappear into the tunnel, never to return. Most of the islands on Lake Titicaca and many of the Power Places have legends about the connecting tunnels. These are called the legends of the chincanas.

We returned to Toribio's house for a midday meal before I left to catch the boat back to Puno. I thanked Toribio for his hospitality and thanked Maximo for all of his special assistance. Maximo invited me to return at any time to explore the many legends of the island.

# All that Glitters

Some months later, I made a return visit with my friends to Amantani. When I arrived, Toribio told me that Maximo had left the island to do some healings on the mainland and would return the next day. I decided to use the day to explore the Island on my own. I climbed to the Temple of the Father, performing the same rituals as Maximo had previously done on the way up the path. When I arrived at the Temple, I found it open but with no other visitor. I had the entire Temple to myself. I went inside and walked to the center of the semi-subterranean level. I was both pleased and surprised to find the large stone covering the entrance to the lower, subterranean level moved. This allowed me to go down in the earth to the lowest level of the Temple. This place held only enough space for one person to stand. While standing in this cavity, the earth's surface was about chest high. I saw a small open door in the side of the earthen wall about waist high.

Next to the opening was a broken ceramic dish, an unusual discovery in these times. Amazingly, in the interior, I observed gold dishes. The sight was dazzling. As I looked at the golden dishes inside of the earthen niche and the broken plain ceramic dish on the outside of the niche, I concluded that I was looking into another dimension of reality. This was the first time I ever experienced visualizing an alternate dimension. I knew in my heart that the "golden" contents of the alternate reality were not to be disturbed. Reverently, I removed myself from this subterranean level of the Temple and gazed at the Lake, trying to understand what I had just witnessed.

As I walked down the mountain, I wondered if someone had entered the Temple unnoticed and opened all the doorways. Perhaps the intruder found the small opening filled with gold and reached in and removed one of the golden dishes. When the dish entered this dimension, the gold dish turned to ceramic. I imagined that when this happened, he dropped the dish and ran. Later, I thought that the contents held in this special place, deep in the Temple of the Father, is gold in nature at a different frequency, but of different materials in this dimension. I decided to keep this experience in my own heart, a lesson that different realities exist within this middle world of experience. The remainder of my visit with Toribio and Maximo was pleasant and rewarding, but not nearly as mystical as my time deep within the Temple. Stranger experiences would greet me on a later trip to Amantani.

# UFO Sighting

Joshua Shapero and I were in Amantani to film some of the sacred sites. He was also seeking crystal skulls. I had told him that I had never heard of any crystal skulls on Amantani or anywhere else, for that matter. Still I enjoyed his company and was happy to accompany him to Amantani. It was about a year and a half since my mystical experience at the Temple. Since then things had been very normal, unusually normal. I was happy to be exploring a new mystery.

Earlier in the day, we climbed the mountains to the area of the two Temples. Joshua had brought a large video camera with him. It was late in the afternoon when we had finished filming. We were walking in silence. I was just feeling the rhythm of my heart and enjoying the walk. Suddenly, we both turned around at the same time. To my astonishment, I saw a large space ship with many small ships hovering behind the larger ship. Later, Joshua said that he counted ten small space ships and the large mother ship. At that moment, neither Joshua nor I could speak. I had a joyous feeling in all of my body. The ships were silver in color. The larger ship was octagonal and domed in its center. The smaller ships were more like discs. My mind told me that, perhaps, my body could not withstand this energy, and I started to worry. With the worry, the ships departed at great speed. Joshua had the presence of mind to try and film the space ships, but nothing recorded. I had no real sense of time, but I think that the encounter was short, yet intense. My conscious mind had responded with normal fear of the unknown, but my knowing heart again responded differently. I tried to find balance with my intellect and my heart, but my heart won, and I walked down the mountain with a sense of excitement and wonder at all that is and all that could be.

Later, I understood more clearly the legend of Runa Antiles and the secret bases for space ships under the mountain ranges. Lake Titicaca is supposed to be one of the entrances. I don't know the answers to these mysteries, but I do know that I had a real experience that afternoon. Amantani remains an island of the mystical and the mysterious.

It helps me, when seeking the understanding of myself within the Cosmos, to know that we are not alone in our spiritual quest. The memory of my unusual experiences at Amantani connects me to many different levels of reality. I am comforted in knowing that I walk my Spiritual Path alone, like the Puma. I am now aware that at the same time, many Light Beings, and even unknown beings, are watching and encouraging me along the way.

# CHARAZANI HEALER

a Paz, the Capital of Bolivia, is my favorite large city. La Paz is the city of Our Lady of Peace. The mountain protector of La Paz is the Apu Lady of Illimani, only a few hours' drive from Puno, south on the Pan American Highway. You enter the area from the mountains and wind your way down into the valley that caresses the sprawling city in the base of this natural bowl-like formation. The city has many sections, but I particularly like the area in the center of the city with the open markets. Of course, La Paz has modern buildings and beautiful shops. You can buy anything that you would need and can remain connected with family and friends by visiting one of the numerous Internet Cafés in the center of the city. The restaurants are also wonderful as well as inexpensive. Since I enjoy good food, I always look forward to visiting La Paz in my travels.

The open market and small shops near San Francisco Square are good places to take tourists. You can buy many different native-made articles in this area. As usual, I am always searching for textiles. Here, you can purchase beautiful new or used textiles, including ponchos and pieces of fabrics that can be worn as shawls or can be used for altar cloths. From my many visits to La Paz, I have become friendly with many of the shop owners. It is always pleasant to see them and catch up on the local news. My friends know that I continually look for the textiles that were made with the natural dyes prior to the 1940's. The colors in these pieces are not as rich as some of the newer fabrics, but they are my favorite. They are also more expensive and not as plentiful, so I treasure them. Occasionally, one piece of fabric will be so beautiful and have such interesting patterns that I will add it to my collection.

In one section of La Paz, a few blocks from San Francisco Square, you can buy all the ingredients for a despacho from the street vendors. The main vendors are at the corner of Santa Cruz and Linares Streets. Here, you can choose from an array of candies of all colors, shapes, and forms. Many candies are symbols of houses, crops, etc. Whatever your intentions, a candy miniature can fulfill the message. You can purchase confetti, candles, colored strings, cotton, gold and silver paper, rice, beans, and coca seeds. It is also necessary to buy a llama fetus and llama fat, which will be wrapped separately, for building and decorating the despacho. You buy different ingredients, depending on your purpose. You purchase ingredients for an offering to Mother Earth that are different from those needed for an offering to the Apus. All of the vendors know what to include and will assist if you tell them the purpose of the offering. I had asked before I made this trip to Bolivia to meet with a Charazani *callawaya*, a special healer, and I knew to bring a despacho of offering for the Apus. I always enjoy visiting this special market, and I particularly like to see if they have any new or unusual items.

I use many textiles as wall hangings at my hotel, Hotel Tapikala in Chucuito, Peru, overlooking Lake Titicaca. In many of the rooms I also display the various knitted hats of the different communities. In each community of the Andes, the men wear a knitted hat that is particular in the design and color pattern to their community. You can recognize the area that a man comes from by simply looking at his hat. I find the many combinations of color and design to be rich in tradition and originality, so I love to display them in the hotel. They add to the color of the rooms and, hopefully, promote interest in their heritage for our foreign guests.

# Mountain Village

The purpose of my trip to Bolivia was not to purchase textiles this time. I was on my way to Charazani, which is located in an area of the Royal Cordillera Mountains and is known for its *callawayas*. These healers are well known by the indigenous communities in Peru, Bolivia, and Chile. They will travel to these areas if they are provided transportation. Otherwise, local people come to them for various healings. Getting to Charazani is a bit easier these days, now that a bus leaves La Paz at five o'clock in the morning on Tuesdays and Fridays, with Charazani being one of its destinations. Only a few years ago, the only way to get there was by car or truck. It is a long bus ride of about eight hours. Most of the road is one lane wide. There are many turns, as the bus labors up and down the sides of the Royal Coldierra Mountains.

The quaint village of Charazani sits on the side of a rather large mountain. It is quite picturesque, with a large village square. I have always enjoyed sitting in the square on the benches under the large trees. The community takes great care of the grass and flowers in the square, which encourages the people to spend a lot of time in the center of the village. Shops of various types line three sides of the square, with the Catholic Church dominating the fourth side. The vista from the village encompasses a deep verdant valley, with a river at its floor, and other neighboring mountains. Hot springs are in an enclosed building a short walk down the one-lane road into the valley. Whenever I walked this road, I would encounter large green hummingbirds playing in the flowers. The flight of the condors is a common sight, but on this visit, I observed six condors flying together, gliding on the air currents that swirled through the mountains.

Once, a small hotel was located near the village square. Since very few visitors come here, the lady who owns the hotel rented out the rooms on a long-term basis. She still serves very delicious food in her small restaurant, the only real restaurant in the village. There is one house that will rent rooms for the night. Young hikers, who are backpacking in this area of the Andes, most often use these sparsely furnished rooms.

Since the village of Charazani is the central village in the region, a military outpost sits at the edge of the village, past the school and near the cemetery. This adds a somewhat more modern flavor to this remote village in Bolivia. On a Friday in late May, I visited Charazani, hoping to spend some time with a very well known and respected healer named Don Daniel. I arrived early in the afternoon to the sound of panpipes and drums. The community was having a fiesta, and everyone in town was participating in some way. The village was very crowded, since many people who now live in La Paz return to their birthplace for the fiesta. Many people danced in the streets. Fortunately, I was able to rent the last available room. The restaurant, unfortunately, was closed.

A lady, who had a small corner shop on the square, agreed to return at seven o'clock and prepare a meal for me. As I walked around the village square after dinner, I talked with the people and discussed buying some of their textiles. Charazani textiles are as well known in the Andes as their healers. I was hoping to purchase some of the older textiles in the form of ponchos or ceremonial bags. Since the Charazani textiles are quite expensive in La Paz, I was hoping to find more reasonable prices in the village. To my surprise and dismay, the people in the village must have heard about the prices in La Paz, because they wanted a considerable amount of money for their handiwork. I left the square empty-handed.

# Flags

A black car with some important-looking people had arrived and parked in front of a one-story plastered house across the small road on the side of the church and near the village square. The only notable item about the house was that it had two flags, one orange and one blue, displayed over its side window. I assumed that the flags represented one of the political parties in Bolivia. When I inquired about the flags and the rather new car parked in front of the house, one of the local men told me that elections were coming up soon and that there was a political rally planned in two days, during the weekly market day when many people would be coming into the village from the outlying areas. The man who owned the house was hosting the rally.

The representatives of the political party hoped to sign up many new members for their party before the election. I was shocked the following morning when I walked to the restaurant, next door to this house, for breakfast. The front of the house had been painted bright orange to match one of the flags! I thought that this man must really be dedicated to his political party to paint his house such a bright orange, when all of the other buildings in the village were earthcolored.

The use of flags has a long history in the Andes. For many years the people in the rural areas could not write, so instead of solely using names, the political parties used different colored flags or painted symbols to distinguish themselves. You will also find, throughout the villages, the use of a flag, often red in color, identifying a house that is selling the local chicha.

# Donkey Dispute

It felt like the middle of the night, but it was with the very first sliver of light in the morning that I was abruptly jarred from my sleep. Two donkeys were in a small enclosure outside by the window of my room. I had seen these donkeys the day before when I arrived. One donkey was a light tan in color and was quite large. The other was darker, shorter and louder. Both had the long hair that the donkeys in the highlands had grown to protect themselves from the cold. It was very cold this morning, especially just before dawn. The donkeys were having an animated conversation that was relentless. One would bray and the other would answer. This was to go on every morning for at least a half hour. While listening to their constant braying, I was not thrilled that the Spaniards had introduced the donkeys to carry heavy loads in the Andes. The llamas are used for carrying many products, but the very heavy loads are packed on the traditional donkey.

I asked the lady at the restaurant, located only a few houses away, about the donkey conversation at breakfast. She laughed and said that the donkeys could never agree on which one of them was the favorite of the family they lived with, and that they had been "arguing" about this for years. If I lived there permanently, I thought, I would have helped to settle the argument or moved the donkeys far from the house. My hostess laughed at my apparent distress and offered me morning tea.

Before I left the restaurant, I inquired about Don Daniel. Some of the local people having breakfast told me that his house was down in the valley, past the hot springs. His house was a short walk along the banks of the river after the road made its turn to ascend the neighboring mountain. I was grateful for the information and grateful that his home was nearby. In the villages, everyone keeps track of everybody else. News travels so quickly by foot that you would think that the people in the village and surrounding areas had telephones!

The people assured me that Don Daniel was not traveling and that I should find him at home. Hector, a young boy of about twelve years, offered to show me the way to Don Daniel's house. I accepted his offer and said that I would meet him in one hour to go and meet Don Daniel. Hector said that, in the meantime, he would tell Don Daniel that I would be visiting him. I was confident that everyone, even the donkeys, would know of my visit by mid-morning.

# Hummingbird vs. Condor

The name *collawaya* means "the one who carries the medicine." Every callaway has his own individual way of conducting a ceremonial offering or a healing. However, certain ingredients are standard in most despachos. I had purchased the basic ingredients for an offering to the Apus when I was in La Paz. I wanted to purchase fresh flowers, tobacco, wine and the local alcohol to take with me to meet Don Daniel, a well-respected callawaya. Hopefully, he would conduct a despacho with me this morning. When I was finished making my purchases, Hector was waiting to escort me to Don Daniel's house. I was sure that I could find it on my own, but I was delighted to walk with him and learn more about the village and surrounding areas.

A half hour into our walk, Hector pointed to an area along the side of the road where two hummingbirds were gathering nectar. The hummingbirds in the Andes are larger than most of the hummingbirds I have seen in the United States. As we watched these two green hummingbirds flit about, I asked Hector if he knew about the time when the hummingbird challenged the condor. He said that he didn't know the story, but asked, "How could a hummingbird, one of the smallest birds, challenge a condor, the largest bird?" "Oh yes," I said, "the hummingbird did challenge the condor. Let me tell you this legend.

"One day in the world of the birds, all the birds were bragging about how strong they were and how high they could fly. The condor noticed these sounds and asked what all this talk was about. One of the falcons told him that the birds were bragging, each saying that they were better than the other. Then all the birds started to say, "We need to hold a competition, and then we will see who is strongest and can fly the highest." The large birds started to practice flying higher and higher in hopes of winning the competition. On the morning of the competition, all the birds gathered to watch the large birds compete to discover who was the best. The condor, who was the largest bird, said that he would give the other birds an advantage to make the competition fair. The smaller birds, like the finches and sparrows, started first. They flew as long and as high as they could. Next the medium-sized birds, the flicker and falcons, took their turn. Of course they flew longer and higher.

"Finally, it was time for the largest birds to fly. The rumor in the skies was that the hummingbird was saying that he could fly longer and higher than any bird, no matter how big they were. All of the large birds laughed at this boast by such a small bird. The condor was the last of the large birds in the competition. The other birds told him of the hummingbird's boast. The condor could hardly stop laughing. The hummingbird was flying nearby with the other little birds who had been watching the larger birds compete. The hummingbird flew into a nearby cloud as the mighty condor spread its wings and started to fly.

"The condor quickly flew up through the clouds, calling 'hummingbird, hummingbird!' The hummingbird was missing. It did not answer. The condor flew higher and higher. The condor flew so high that he couldn't see any other birds. He was calling to the other birds and laughing. The condor was confident that he had flown higher than any other bird. He called out in a loud voice, 'Who's the best, who's the best?' Suddenly, the hummingbird replied, 'I am the best because I am the highest.' The hummingbird had climbed onto the top of the condors collar of feathers unnoticed when the condor flew through the clouds." Hector laughed at the thought of the hummingbird tricking the condor in this way. I ended the story saying, "So don't ever be too confident like the condor. Remember that even the smallest ones can do great things."

When we reached the house, I rewarded Hector with colored pencils that I had purchased in the village. He was delighted, and we parted company. When I knocked on the door of the adobe brick house situated about twenty feet from the river, a diminutive man with a gentle face and endearing smile greeted me. Don Daniel was less than five feet tall and slight in build. Of course, Hector had alerted him to my intentions of visiting this morning. Don Daniel had coca tea ready. After our greetings, we sat down and drank tea together. I asked Don Daniel if he would make an offering to the Apus for me that morning. His reply was both positive and negative. He told me that he would be happy to have a despacho to the Apu Akamani for me, but the best time for the offering was late in the afternoon. Don Daniel said that he was glad to have my company for the day and that we could end our visit with the burning of the despacho.

# Struck by Lightning

As we walked on the path by the river, I asked Don Daniel how he had become a healer. He laughed, and said, "I did not want to be a healer. When I was a boy, my godfather, who was a healer himself, told me that I was a healer. I told him that I wasn't interested in being a healer. After my schooling, I went to work in the silver mines. I led a normal life until the day that I was struck by the lightning. I guess I was in my mid-twenties at the time. I don't know the exact year I was born, but I was still in my twenties when this occurred. I was in a coma for about a week. My godfather continuously prayed over me on a daily basis. I gradually recovered from the coma, but I had many after-effects, and I could not function very well. After another week, I went to my godfather and asked for another healing for the after-effects. My godfather said that he had done all that he could and that I would have to heal myself. Well, I had no other choice. I prayed and performed ceremonies for many days.

Over the period of a couple of weeks, I regained all of my strength and health and I was able to resume my regular life. After this happened, people declared me a healer and came to me for assistance." "This is an incredible story," was my reply. "What kind of healings do you perform?" I asked. "Well," he responded, "I have added to my types of healings over the years. I pray for all types of physical healings and perform despachos to the Apus for these healings. I also work with unwanted entities that can take over a person. Just last month, a man came from Puno and took me to his home to heal his son. His son was a young man, not quite twenty years old, who went into the mountains and became possessed with an entity. I worked with the young man for many days of prayers and offerings. When I left, he returned to his normal self. I told the father to come for me again if the entity returned. I have not heard from him, so I assume that his son is well and the healing was permanent."

# Reading the Future

After giving me a brief history of his heritage as a callawaya, Don Daniel then offered to do a reading for me with the coca leaves. We walked over to an area near the river that had a flat stone that could serve as a mesa. Don Daniel placed a piece of textile over the stone and proceeded to place two hands-full of coca leaves on the textile. He began an invocation to the Apus and to various Catholic Saints. At random, Don Daniel plucked coca leaves from the pile and spread them over the textile. He started to speak immediately regarding the energy and the messages from Mama Coca. He first gave me a general reading and then asked if I had any questions.

Don Daniel told me that I would return to Charazani, and that I would be successful in my business endeavors, as well as in my spiritual quest. I was pleased with this message and had no further questions. Don Daniel then asked me to make some offerings to the Apus. After the reading, Don Daniel and I sat and discussed it. He said to me, "Jorge Luis this was a very favorable reading, indicating that you will have a great deal of success." "Yes," I replied, "I am very pleased with this forecast for me." Don Daniel continued, "It is important for all of our people to walk well on both paths, the material and the physical. There is abundance in the universe, and it is advisable to have abundance in all areas of the life here. It would be good for all the people to see someone who is successful in business also very devoted to the spiritual. I think our young people think that they must make a choice between the two. They need to recognize that you can have material success and still keep the spiritual life that is your heritage."

"I agree," I said, "Sometimes it is very tricky to walk on both paths at once. If you stay true first to the spiritual and follow your heart, the material aspect will flourish. If you ignore the heritage of who you are and do not live your spiritual beliefs, you may have material success, but your heart and spirit will wither." Don Daniel smiled and said, "We agree on many things my friend. I think that we will have a very successful despacho this afternoon."We walked back to Don Daniel's house to drink some coca tea. While we were having tea, I noticed hunks of metal sitting on a textile in the corner of the room. I inquired about the purpose of the metal. "Oh, the pieces of lead!" Don Daniel replied, as he went over and brought a piece back for me to hold. The metal was cold to the touch and very heavy. "We use this metal to read a person's health. Would you like to have a reading of your health?" Of course, my answer was yes.

Don Daniel took the large piece of metal and put it into the fire while he boiled water. In a few moments, the water was boiling and the hunk of metal was very hot. Don Daniel picked up the piece of metal from the fire with a tong-like tool and dropped the metal into the pot of boiling water. Streams of seemingly liquid metal separated from the large piece of metal and formed a unique swirl of metal on the surface of the water. This pattern is what Don Daniel read. The only area of concern in my health was my kidneys. According to this famous callaway, I would only need to drink more water daily and drink a special mineral water on occasion to restore my kidneys to perfect health. Again, I was pleased with this reading. This was the first time I had seen such a reading, but I had full confidence in this gentle yet powerful healer. I made a mental note of his recommendations and promised myself that I would heed his advice.

# Herbal Remedies

The callawayas are also known for their long journeys to do healings. They collect herbs from all of the regions of the coast, the jungle, and the mountains. The Charazani callawayas regularly visit these regions in Chile, Argentina, Bolivia, and Peru. They are recorded as having traveled as far as the Panama Canal when it was being built, and there was much reported sickness. They are considered masters in their knowledge of herbal remedies. The callawaya trade herbs that they gather from all of the regions and various countries they visit. The knowledge of how to make the herbal remedies is handed down from one callawaya to another. Don Daniel, who was struck by lightening in becoming a healer, acquired his knowledge about healing energies from within his own heart and mind. When asked about the herbs, he said that he learned much from his Godfather, who was a callawaya and from other healers in different locations. There are hundreds of herbal plants and remedies. Being a callawaya requires both a great deal of study and inherent healing power.

In their travels, the callawayas will charge an appropriate amount of money for their readings, their ceremonies, and their remedies. While some spend time in La Paz, most of the Charazani healers practice their art at home or on long pilgrimages throughout the four countries, wherever they are invited or feel needed.

# Twelve Dishes

When I arrived at Don Daniel's house, I had brought all of the ingredients for a despacho. During the morning, Don Daniel had said that the best time for the despacho was in the late afternoon. Since it was now approaching sunset, Don Daniel retrieved my gifts and began to prepare a mesa in his house for the despacho. His assistant arrived, and we were introduced. His name was Carlos, and he was studying with Don Daniel.

The first thing that was placed on the mesa table was the textile in the traditional Charazani colors and designs. This particular textile was very old and made from natural dyes, so the colors were subdued. This fabric was probably never washed so that the power it absorbed would not be lost. By the looks of this fabric, it was very powerful! While Don Daniel was spreading the altar cloth, Mario was preparing the flowers by pulling the blooms from the stems of the red and white carnations and sorting the petals into piles, according to color. Next, Don Daniel placed twelve shells in rows of three across the top of the covered mesa. He explained that the shells are the dishes of the Mother Earth or the Apukunas. They are also symbols of Mama Cocha, the lake of origin, and the sea. Carlos started to select the kintuis and place them on a separate textile. Don Daniel directed me to put a kintui in each shell with an intention or prayer. It was acceptable to put more than one kintui in each shell, according to the number of intentions.

Carlos then brought the *wira khoa*, a highland plant that has natural oil that the people believe is the fat of the Mother Earth. Wira khoa is aromatic when burned. Don Daniel added a small piece of the plant, followed by a piece of llama fat, in each shell. Mario presented Don Daniel with the red and white carnation petals. Petals of each color were placed in each shell in the same ritualistic fashion. Candies in many shapes and bright colors were then placed on top to complete the colorful and meaningful design of each of the twelve shells. The completed mesa was one of the most colorful that I had ever observed.

Don Daniel then took great care to "dress" the llama fetus. First, he covered it with cotton that he secured with multicolored string. He then wove the flower petal into the string to create a beautiful effect. This was the best-dressed llama fetus that I had seen at an offering, and I had seen many. I was impressed with the precision and gentleness that Don Daniel expressed throughout the ceremony.

Wine along with a local white alcohol, was sprinkled in sequence on the each shell as well as on the fetus but with a much larger clamshell. Throughout this ritual, Don Daniel was praying. Mario then offered Don Daniel and me a cigarette to smoke. In this part of the ritual, you blow the heavy energy out of the left side of your mouth as you exhale the smoke. From the right side of your mouth, you blow your intentions. Together, we then chewed coca leaves. In completing the ceremony, Don Daniel emptied the contents of the shells into a large ceramic bowl. He held it over my head as he prayed for my intentions.

We then proceeded into the yard where Mario had started a fire in the special location for the burning of the offering. Don Daniel asked me to pour the contents of the bowl onto the fire. Unlike the Q'ero, who do not watch Pachamama eat, the people from Charazani watch the burning of the offering until it is complete. As the fire finished, we performed a challa by throwing a shell-full of wine into the fire and then returned to the mesa.

In conclusion, Don Daniel blessed me by holding the llama fetus over my head and praying for me. He told me to take the llama fetus to my house. Don Daniel smiled and said to me, "Bury the llama near the entrance of your house. He will act as your lawyer, your defense." I graciously accepted the llama fetus. This may sound strange to people who are not from the Andes, but it is a common practice to bury a llama fetus on your property for protection. It is also believed that the llama will carry your intentions to the Mother Earth and the Apus. Don Daniel asked me to join him in a meal before we parted.

# Amulets and Talismans

Charazani has specially designed alabaster stones. The callawaya carve unique designs for each person, and they are not interchangeable. They are carved for the purposes and intentions of that individual person. Certain basic designs are used for married people, and other basic designs are used for single people. There are many designs, and one person could have a variety of these stones carved for them by a callawaya. Most of the stones have geometric designs and anthropomorphic designs. Most of these healers begin their carving with an equilateral triangle because this symbol is a protector from negativity and unwanted entities. They are not sure of the origin of the design, colonial or Incan. The callaawaya are as strong in their Catholic Faith as they are in their native traditions. That evening, Don Daniel carved a beautiful alabaster stone with a unique design and then presented it to me as a gift.

I felt overwhelmed with gratitude. I added this stone to my personal mesa. I accepted this beautiful stone, containing the powerful love of Don Daniel carved into it, to travel with me, as a protector, on my unfolding spiritual quest as a chacaruna.

# SACRED VALLEY OF THE INCAS

The Willca Mayu River glides through the valley with majestic dignity as it greets each mountain Apu. The Apus are steadfast in overlooking its wanderings, with unspoken respect. This Sacred River of the Incas originates high in the Wilcanota Mountains and proceeds in a steady flow of pristine water down through the lush valley. It becomes the Urubamba River, which curls around Machu Picchu in its journey to the Amazon. Majestic mountains cradle the valley that contains the length of the continuous Sacred River. Scattered within this Sacred Valley, following the path of the Urubamba River, are most of the Sacred Sites of the Incas, both discovered and undiscovered.

Urubamba means "fields of Light." This is one of the *bambas*, the fields that connects with the sacred space. Apubamba refers to the "fields of the Apus," which are located in the highlands, while Willcabamba refers to the "fields of God" which are located in the mountains and valleys near Machu Picchu. In the Inca tradition, all of these fields reflect the Upper World, which also includes the Milky Way. We have approximately ninety-five Power Places, or Sacred Sites, in the Sacred Valley. Each of these sites is connected to a particular constellation in the Milky Way, which is the Sacred River in the sky in the Andean tradition. The Urubamba is seen as a mirror reflection of the Milky Way, as a Sacred River on the Mother Earth.

The *amautas* (teacher) or *yachas* (one who knows) were the wisdom-keepers in ancient times. They had the ability to read the solar memory. They were the ones who read the expressions of Mother Earth in synchronicity with the Milky Way. In relatively recent times, the past fifteen or twenty years, many people "remembered" that the Sacred Sites correlated to particular stars in the Milky Way. They also remembered that all of the Sacred Valley was a reflection of the Milky Way.

# Solar Expressions

n 1992, I started to celebrate the solstices and equinoxes at Ollantaytambo in the Sacred Valley. One of the tour guides who knew me and knew that I was from the region of Lake Titicaca asked, "Why did you come to the Sacred Valley for the celebrations instead of attending the celebrations at the Lake?" I told Dante that, "I am following in the footsteps of my ancestors," and I showed him the face of Tunupa, a Master from Lake Titicaca, whose face is naturally formed and carved high on the mountain overlooking Ollantaytambo. I then pointed out the face of Tunupa for my friend. What is interesting about Tunupa's face is that it changes expression from the sunlight to the shade. I explained to Dante that I was very interested in the sunlight on Ollantaytambo at these special times of the year. He invited me to have dinner with him and return at night to gaze at the stars high above the lights near the Temple of the Wind. I accepted the invitation, and we left for his house.

The night turned out to be extremely clear. The moon was only a crescent, so the Milky Way and the constellations dominated the sky. The feeling was otherworldly as Dante, his son Broz, age ten, and I climbed the many ancient stone steps to the flat area up by the Temple of the Wind. Dante pointed out the Southern Cross, which was high in the sky, as we spread a blanket out as our observatory. I asked Broz if he could see the llama flying in the sky. "Where is the llama?" he asked. First, I pointed out the eye of the llama, the stars of alpha and beta centaurs, which shone brilliantly near the Southern Cross. I sat next to him and traced the head and body and folded legs of the llama around the black cloud that is so prominent in the mists of the Milky Way. "In the Andean world we call this constellation the Flying Llama," I answered. "Just in the rainy season, the Llama flies to the sea to drink the water. Then the llama returns and releases the water to fall to the earth as rain to nourish the crops,"

I asked Broz, "Do you know the name of the moon?" "Of course, it is Mama Killa," was his immediate answer. "Do you know why the moon is called Mama?" I queried. "I don't know it's just the name," Broz replied with a nonchalant nod. I engaged his eyes and said, "Well the name is important. We call the moon Mama because in the Upper World, the Sun is the Father and the moon is the feminine complement. There is always the balance of the duality of the masculine and the feminine." Broz shrugged and smiled, saying, "If you say so." I smiled and hoped that someday Broz would be more interested in Mama Killa.

Dante then pointed out Orion to his son, showing him the shoulders, legs, belt, and sword. I asked Dante, "Did you know that Orion, like the Southern Cross, was a chacana, a bridge?" Dante said, "I have heard this expression, but I never paid attention to its meaning." Broz asked me, "How can stars be a bridge?" "They are a bridge, a bridge to the other side of the Milky Way," I replied in my best storytelling voice to keep his attention. "The Milky Way is a river in the sky. From the ancestors we know that Orion and the Southern Cross are the stars that form a bridge over the Sacred River, the Milky Way. The Ccoto, the Pleiades, are guides that will tell you how cold it will be on the crossing." "What is on the other side of the Milky

Way?" asked the now curious Broz. "It is a mystery, but the legend says that the Milky Way is the bridge for the spirit to return home," was my answer. I added, "Many people believe that you can receive energy from the stars." Broz had more questions, but Dante thought that it was time for him to return to his present home, since he had to get up for school in the morning. I stopped for a moment before we left to appreciate the beauty of the night.

On another visit, I met with the Elorieta brothers, who showed me where the sunlight awakens the llama and activates the pyramid. The early people built terraces shaped like a pyramid following the natural formation of Mother Earth. The overall result was the formation of a landscape representation of the llama, as seen from the top of Ollantaytambo, at the place of the Temple to the Wind. The first light strikes the landscape llama, another power animal symbol, indicating service to mankind in the Kay Pacha. The sun, Inti, is the main architect of the initial expression of beauty. The Elorieta brothers, who later published a book on the Sacred Valley, introduced me to the solar wonderment of Ollantaytambo. Reflecting on the events of the day, I realized that all of the Sacred Sites were a reflection of the Milky Way and connected to the solstices and equinoxes.

# Don Miguel's Visit

More than ten years ago, I received a phone call from Gini Gentry, who was an apprentice to Don Miguel Ruiz, a Toltec *nagual*, who resides in the United States and has many students and followers. Since I first met Don Miguel, he has published many books, including the wonderful book, *The Four Agreements*. Gini asked me to organize a tour of Peru for Don Miguel and his group of about thirty-five people. At the time, I had not heard of Don Miguel, but I was happy to escort this group to the Sacred Sites in Cusco region and the Sacred Valley. I went to Lima to meet the group at the International Airport. This man, Don Miguel, was very humble and took great care of all the people traveling with him. I was impressed with him and looked forward to the two weeks we would have together. We had scheduled six days in the Crystal City, Machu Picchu, alone. We flew in a local airplane to Cusco. We immediately boarded a bus headed to the town of Urubamba, where it was warm, beautiful, and at a lower altitude, to ease the group's adjustment to the area.

On the bus, I gave the group a briefing about the area and our pilgrimage throughout the Inca lands. I introduced them to our concept of Apus, as Light Beings that live on the snow-capped mountains. Don Miguel joined the conversation, adding his knowledge. When I asked him how he knew about the Apus, he explained that he could access the information from the Cosmos. I was amazed by the detail of the knowledge he had. I realized that I was in the presence of a man who had reached the high state of consciousness that we call "Tucuy Yachainiyoc," the one who has the wisdom. We stopped along the road where we could see some of the Apus. The beautiful place had a clear view of the Apu Sawasiray and Apu Pitusiray. When we assembled in a small clearing near the bus, I showed Don Miguel how to make a kintui. We blew our intentions of love onto the coca leaves and offered our love and recognition to the Apus.

Don Miguel then lectured about love, and how to express that love without reserve. He asked everybody to express his or her love freely to the Mother Earth. We then all kissed the earth and placed each side of our face on the Pachamama. I quickly realized that the Inca and Toltec traditions and beliefs were similar in essence and similar in understanding. Our next stop was the Alambra Hotel, where Don Miguel held a seminar on the "Four Agreements." Don Miguel used every moment and every opportunity to teach his students. As his newest student, I was anxious to hear every word Don Miguel uttered. It was a privilege for me to accompany him and learn from him, as I introduced him to the Sacred Sites of my heritage.

# Urco

The first Power Place we visited was Urco. One of the favorite activities of Don Miguel when we arrived at a new Sacred Site was to use the energy of the place to activate each person's own energy source. Urco is a small but very powerful place in a beautiful valley in the midst of the fields. At this place, a large rock has a distinctive carving of a snake, encircling almost half of the rock. A channel forms the body of the snake and it ends at the carved head of the snake. Some people also see the face of the puma in the face of the snake. The line of the channel also can be seen as the bill of the condor that is present in a larger picture of the landscape rock formation. At the top of the rock, an indentation is seen as the eye of the condor. When the indication is filled with water, it serves as a mirror observatory of the Milky Way.

Don Miguel appeared to be quite comfortable here. This is a private place that is hidden and only known to the local people. This was my first visit to this beautiful site. The power at this place seemed intense yet peaceful for me. I imagine that Don Miguel also enjoyed the power he experienced here, for he spent the afternoon teaching and conversing with his students. In some way, Don Miguel introduced me to Urco, in that he asked me to find an outdoor, private place where he could spend time with his students. I asked the local people where I might take such a large group nearby that fit this description. They led us to Urco.

I have returned to Urco many times since I first went with Don Miguel. This place was of great interest to me, so I spent time with the local people researching the oral legends surrounding this site. They told me two or three legends regarding the enchantment of the stone. I went back and tried to read the rock. The rock told me that this was a place for ceremonies. The rock went on to tell me that in each ceremony, Mama Sara, the spiritual mother of corn and material food, and Mama Coca, the spiritual mother of coca and spiritual food, were to be honored. Mama Sara and Mama Coca are favorite daughters of Pachamama and are always ready to be of service.

The rock then revealed that chicha was to be poured into its channel so that the flow of the chicha would start at the tail of the snake and wind around the rock to pour over the edge of the rock at the head of the snake. Then I was told to place kintuis of coca leaves with intentions of gratitude and messages to the Mother Earth in the flow of the chicha at the back of the snake. The rock also told me that I could read how well the offering was accepted by Pachamama by which side of the coca leaves was apparent when it landed on the Mother Earth. In my heart, I knew that it would be important to offer incense to the Upper World and the rock itself during the ceremony. Later, I was to perform this ceremony with many groups at Urco. I thank Don Miguel for "leading" me to this special place when I was introducing him to the Sacred Sites.

# Pisac

igh on the side of a mountain, overlooking an expansive lush valley that is surrounded by two mountains converging in the distance, are the remains of an ancient stone Incan temple. This is the Sacred Site of Pisac. You have to walk up a steep incline to the area of the temple. This temple has many rooms. My favorite room has twenty-one niches, three times seven, that could have housed the power tools or sacred symbols of the Incan priests. As with all the Sacred Sites, Pisac has the symbol of the chacana, the four-sided cross with three levels. In Pisac, the chacana is formed from one stone that is placed outside the courtyard of the temple. In certain sunlight, the chacana stone's shadow projects the perfect form of the sacred symbol. The stonework of this temple is outstanding. It reflects not only the art of architecture, but also the art of sculpture in connection with the Cosmos. Within what would have been the walls of the temple is a "hitching post to the sun," a large stone set in a formation of smaller carved stones that could have been the center of the Temple to the Sun. Like in other Sacred Sites, the Temple at Pisac had many temples within the Temple.

A stone archway is still standing that ushers you into another large room, or courtyard, that holds many people. Further up the mountain, there is another stone temple that I named the Temple of the Condor because a room seems to represent the body of the condor. Then two stone walls form the wings of the condor. Looking out from the body of the condor, you are visually greeted by the lush valley and the distant mountains. Looking out from here spiritually, you are greeted by the Apus. This is a perfect setting for the ceremony of aura (energy field of the body) cleansing with the feathers of the condor and incense, palo santo. In this ceremony, we move the energy surrounding the person's body to release any heavy energy from their "energetic body." This is done with a whipping motion, using a male or female condor feather, around the physical body. The Apus accept and release this energy into the Cosmos for its transmutation into light energy. This is a similar ritual to the burying of the heavy energy in an offering to Mother Earth for transmutation of the heavy energies.

I arrived at Pisac with Don Miguel and his group of students at sunset. We came to the Temple at this hour to visit the Site and to hold a fire ceremony. The sunset is considered the perfect time for holding a ceremony of gratitude for the day, for the life, and for all the gifts from the Cosmos. As we stood on the mountainside, Don Miguel showed his students how to look into the sun and see a tunnel of light coming from the sun. He then pointed out that the color of the sun at this moment was really black. The colors around the tunnel of light were pink, blue, and yellow. This was certainly a new perspective for me in viewing the sun at sunset. As the light from the sun diminished, Don Miguel walked through all the areas of the Temple, communing with the priest and priestesses, whose energies were still present. Most of the people in the group could actually feel the presence of the ancestors. We walked in Pisac for about an hour before the fire ceremony.

# Fire Ceremony

Days before we arrived at Pisac, during the seminar at the Alambra Hotel, Don Miguel began the preparation for the fire ceremony. He talked extensively about the heavy energies, such as guilt, fear, and regret. Every student was asked to search their heart for what heavy energies they were carrying with them. Don Miguel then asked the students to make masks with art materials to represent these huchas. Some students made many masks. For my part, I gathered the wood and purchased some flowers and special oils to use in the ceremony. I was curious about the masks that the students constructed with personal care. The time between the making of the masks and the night of the ceremony provided the students time to reflect on their heavy energies, as well as prepare to release them during the ceremony.

A few moments before the ceremony was to begin, Don Miguel invited me to walk with him a few yards away from the group. As we walked toward the Temple of the Sun, Don Miguel stopped and looked directly at me as he said, "You have been a priest in this place in the Incan times. This ceremony is well known to you, and you will conduct the fire ceremony tonight." I felt privileged to receive this information, especially since it came from Don Miguel. It was an honor to conduct the fire ceremony for this extraordinary Tucay Yachainiyoc.

I started the ceremony, invoking the four directions. This is a ritual, inviting the four winds to come to this ceremony in this place. I learned this ritual from the shamans in the north of Peru. The wind from the East, the place of the sunrise, has the condor as its power animal. We asked of the East to teach us how to fly with the Pacha. We asked the wind of the South, with the power animal amaru, the great serpent, to teach us how to shed our sorrows and our guilty feelings. We asked the wind of the West, with the power animal of the puma, or jaguar, to help us face our death, our greatest fear. Finally, we asked the wind of the North, with the power animal of the hummingbird, to carry our gratitude to the ancestors, the grandfathers and grandmothers. Then I invited the Apukunas from many regions to join us in our ceremony by calling out their names in a loud voice. Using the coca leaves, we asked the Guardians of the Place and the ancestors for permission to hold the fire ceremony.

The fire was burning nicely when I began the ceremony by offering flowers to the fire. I asked the fire to bless all the intentions of the people participating in the ritual. The people formed a circle around the fire and proceeded to chant and dance for a few moments. One by one, the students came and threw their masks, symbolizing their heavy energy, into the burning fire. Each person burned his or her mask, giving the heavy energy to Pachamama to be transformed in the fire. We stood around the fire until it consumed all of the masks and the last flame, the spirit of the fire, was extinguished. In closing, we hugged and congratulated each other for the commitment of releasing the heavy energies and becoming our authentic selves.

# Ollantaytambo

The morning following the fire ceremony, we went to Ollantaytambo. As we arrived, we again asked permission of the Guardian to enter this Sacred Space with coca leaves. I lead the group for a cleansing at the sacred fountain, where there is a chacana in the rock that has the three expressions of the three levels. We went to the astronomical center to calculate the time by the position of the shadow on the ancient lines carved for this purpose. On the way to the Condor Temple, Don Miguel stopped at a particular rock that he felt was a doorway to the Cosmos. He said that we could read the message of the Cosmos in the rock. Everyone placed their hands with open palms, as well as their faces and bodies, on the rock and went inside the rock. Many people had mystical experiences as they meditated on the rock. Some people received messages, while others experienced a wonderful feeling of connectedness with the rock. The Condor Temple is to the right of the fountain and is marked by a replica of a condor with a collar in the stone of the side of the mountain.

The group gathered and "flew" within ourselves, viewing our lives without judgment, just as the condor sees very near and very far the perfection of creation, without judgment. After this experience, the group was open to seeing the Inca in the profile of the mountain with the Mascay Pacha, or band, around his head. The Mascay Pacha means looking for the Essence of the Cosmos.

We left the Temple of the Condor and walked the many stone steps up the left side of Ollantaytambo to the Temple of the Wind. This Temple sits high in the air on the edge of a cliff. It is thought to be pre-Incan in time. It is unusual because it is constructed of huge stones that were quarried on the other side of the river. How they got these stones up to this high ledge is still a mystery. It was here in the rushing currents of wind that Don Miguel spent time teaching his students to "let go" or "fly" as they confronted their fears. I pointed out the landscape pyramid with the mystical llama to Don Miguel and the group. They marveled at the beauty and spiritual significance of the valley below them. I then asked them to raise their gaze past the river and upward to the right to view the Apu Yanantin. This is a mountain with two peaks, very near to each other, symbolizing the union of two dissimilar energies. Don Miguel stood silently as he seemed to absorb the beauty and spiritual significance of the majestic surroundings of Ollantaytambo.

# Moray

Behind the Sacred Valley on the road from Chinchero to Urubamba is the Sacred Site of Moray. Archeologists tell us that this was the place for agriculture experimentation. It is unusual architecture that starts in a flat circle and continues to form concentric circles in terraces upward from the flat center circle, which has a radius of about fifteen meters. Each terrace is about two meters high and four meters in depth. Seven levels of terraces are in this main circle formation. At the top of the seventh level there is a flat area before other smaller circle formations occur.

We arrived at Moray late in the morning. The bus ride had taken about two hours, and the last portion of the road was very bumpy. Everyone was happy to get off the bus and walked around a bit before we went over to the actual site. I had described Moray to Don Miguel, and he had prepared for the students a special exercise that would take advantage of the topography and power of the site. We gathered the group and began to walk down the path to the flat area on the top of the seventh level of the terraces. Don Miguel was impressed with the configuration of the main circle. Scattered around the entire flat upper level were stones of various sizes, many in piles. The group was divided into small groups of five or six students. Each group was to work together to again cleanse themselves of the heavy energies and release the energy into the stones. The small groups spent about twenty minutes to half an hour on this ritual. Don Miguel then led the entire group into the center of the bottom flat circle.

Don Miguel began the descent in a spiral downward, with the students following in a single continuous line of people. At each level, Don Miguel stopped and asked permission to continue the descent, activating the power of each level. The effect of this ritual was that each person went deeper into their own mind and their own heart at each level. When we reached the bottom circle, we were in various altered states of consciousness. Beautiful chanting from a tape recorder was played as the group arrived and assembled in the circle. A small dish was placed in the middle of the earthen circle to burn the incense of *palo santo*. Each student was invited to dig deep within his or her heart and expand his or her consciousness in harmony with the Cosmic Spiral. The ceremony was moving.

After the ceremony, when we returned to the area at the top of the terraces, I overheard Don Miguel explaining to his students the position of his hands when he was activating the energy on the descent. He held his right hand up to demonstrate the formation of the fingers. The fingers next to the thumb were held upward, while the other two fingers were folded into the palm, as was the thumb. The two fingers folded into the palm represented water and earth. The two fingers pointed upward represented fire and air. I believe that the thumb represented the etheric. Don Miguel commented that the Master Jesus often held his right hand in this manner. It was in our Inca teachings that the right hand activates energy and that the left hand receives energy, but I had never heard the explanation of the fingers before. I was grateful to learn this information.

I returned to Moray with groups many times after this day with Don Miguel. After learning from Don Miguel so many beautiful concepts, I was able to expand my ceremonial use of this Sacred Site. Sometimes I would work with seven charkas or energy centers of the body on the terraces. Other times, I would work with the seven rays of color on the individual terraces. Always, I would hold gratitude in my heart to Don Miguel for our time together at Moray.

# Cusco

itting at an altitude of 11,000 feet in the Andean valley, and located near the Sacred Valley, is Cusco, the Capital of the ancient Inca Territory. Like all of the Andean cultures, the capital of each culture or civilization was considered a "navel," a "vital center." In pre-Incan times, Cusco was known as Aqa Mama, or Mama Chicha. Other ancient capitals were Chupin of the Chavin culture and the pre-Incan capital of Tiawanaku, which was originally called Tapikala, meaning "central stone." Cusco was purposefully designed as a solar city that is activated by the solstices and equinoxes. The street plan follows the pattern of a puma. On the winter solstice of June twenty-first, the rising sun first kisses the tail and the head of the Puma with a ray of light. Then the sun activates the energy of the city by lighting each street, individually and in sequence, that is facing the sunrise within the body of the puma. Underneath the city of Cusco, the researchers have found many tunnels, and some are theorizing that there may be another entire city under the present city of approximately half a million people.

In the Inca tradition, Cusco is located at a crossroads of ley lines and is in a prominent position on the most major ley line that progresses northward from Tiawanaku, Amantani, and Pukara, to Cusco. Originally, Cusco was divided by its Inca founders into two parts to indicate the flow between the dualities, masculine and feminine. The upper part, representing the masculine aspect, was called Hanan Qosqo, and the lower part, representing the feminine aspect, was called Hurin Qosqo. A legend states that the Father Sun sent Mallcu Capac and Mama Ocllo, the first Incas, to the Kay Pacha to organize the people living on Mother Earth.

These original Incas arose out of Lake Titicaca and proceeded to Cusco. They brought knowledge and civilization to the people. The Incas understood the difference between the physical and metaphysical, but considered them both to be part of the Oneness. In the Andean world, we do not understand the separation of the spirit and matter. Life is comprised of the energy, *kawsay*, that permeates all of Creation on different vibrational levels. It is believed by some that Mallcu Capac and Mama Ocllo brought the Inca Laws and the knowledge of planting, harvesting, and weaving to the people. Cusco became the center of the four regions of the Incas, called Tawantinsuyo. As the influence of the Incas grew in the regions, Cusco thrived as a cultural, economic, and spiritual hub of the Children of the Sun.

# Golden Disc

The Incas built one major temple on their expansive Main Square in Cusco. The temple was named Coricancha. This was one of the temples that astounded the Spanish when they captured Cusco. The Inca used gold to make offering dishes and replicas of all forms of life. All of the animal and vegetable kingdom was formed in gold life-sized figures. Never had the Spaniards seen this quantity of gold in one place nor the quality of workmanship with gold. The Incas only used gold for ceremonial purposes and valued it for its beauty, not for any monetary value. Their most precious treasure was made of gold. It was the Golden Disc that hung in a temple some blocks from the main square. We can see the remains of where the disc hung in the present day church of Santo Domingo.

According to legend, the Golden Disc is a physical representation of the Sun, the central Sun, and it was made with special gold. It was not valued for the gold, it was valued for its meaning. The legend says that the Golden Disc had a special vibration that could activate the powers inherent in each person. When the Incas heard that the Spanish had landed on the continent, they wanted to protect the Golden Disc over all else. They took the Golden Disc to Lake Titicaca and lowered it into the Lake for its protection. No one knows the exact location of the Disc in the Lake.

The Golden Disc can be experienced in many ways and on many levels. I personally had one unusual experience when I was meditating with a group of about twelve people on a grassy clearing overlooking the Sacred Lake on Moon Island. It was a clear afternoon, with no clouds in the sky. We were just starting a ceremony and invoking the names of all of Divinity. One of the group members interrupted the ceremony to point out a light in the shape of a disc that was high in the sky over the lake. When I looked in the indicated direction, I did see the distinct ray of light in the shape and size of the Golden Disc. I felt in my heart that this was a physical expression of the Golden Disc. When we returned to the ceremony, many of us felt that our energy flow was greater and that the ceremony was exceptional in its impact. One of the group sent me a photograph showing the group and the disc of light in the background. This picture fits with the legend that says that the physical Golden Disc represents another Golden Disc from the ancient continent of Lemuria. It is said that this Lemurian Golden Disc usually vibrates and manifests in the fourth dimension. It can be experienced only when you expand your consciousness.

# Vibrant Marketplace

Cusco today is a bustling city that caters to many tourists from around the world. While you can easily find an Internet Cafe, Cusco has retained its charm because many of the residents still wear their native garb. The heart of the city is the Main Square, Hucay Pata, and site of two major Catholic Churches. The cathedral is built over an Incan temple. At certain times, you can visit an area below the present church and see the large round ancient stones of the Incas, called cuya. Many visitors to the city go to the cathedral to see the beauty of the colonial Spanish religious art, as well as the beauty of the mysterious ancient stones.

Many restaurants open onto this square. On one side of the square, opposite the cathedral, begins the marketplace for the tourists. Throughout this area that stretches for a few blocks and connects to the second square, the Cusi Pata, are art and handicrafts of the region. The people are happy to barter since many vendors are selling the same products. On all the side streets, a multitude of shops sell clothing, jewelry, crystals, etc., in all price ranges. If you are interested in the handicrafts and art of the Andean culture, Cusco is a shopper's paradise.

Don Miguel and his group had one day of free time in Cusco. Most of the group went on a river rafting tour and had a wonderful day on the water. Others visited some of the Incan sites in the Cusco Valley, such as Sacsayhuaman, Quenco, Pucapucara, Tambomachay, Illapata, and Xzone. Everyone enjoyed their free day, which of course included some shopping. The next day we left for Tipon.

# Tipon

It is more than twenty kilometers to Tipon, but the road is paved so the bus ride was pleasant. On the way I explained to the group that Tipon is the major Temple of the Water. In earlier times, this Sacred Site was notable in that each rising spring made different vibrational sounds. The Site also distinguishes the masculine and feminine aspects of water. As mentioned earlier, water that is falling vertically is masculine, and water that lies or flows horizontally is feminine.

Water is representative of the flowing of the red water, the blood, through the physical body to sustain life, and the flowing of the white water, the mother's milk, to the breast to sustain the infant. Spiritually, the water is seen as a denser form of light that is alive with the radiation of the Sun's gifts to the Kay Pacha. The basis of life is water. You can connect and work on an energetic level through the energy present in the waters of the lakes, the rivers, and the springs.

We left the bus in the parking area and climbed the short pathway up to the springs of Tipon. The Cultural Institute of Peru has been rebuilding Tipon. They have created walls of cut stone that channel the waters from the springs onto terraces that allow the water to flow only down particular channels to the next level. On the top level of the spring, there are four channels that allow the water to flow in a fan-like pattern to the next level in which the water has full range of movement as it proceeds down to the next level. The water flows down many terraces before it joins the earthen terraces and is channeled down one side of their grass and stone terraces. This was one of the major hydraulic installations for the people in the area.

In an area still under construction, the waters poured freely and abundantly over a ridge in a narrow yet forceful six-foot waterfall. This was the area of Tipon that appealed to Don Miguel. He led his students in a ceremony of a new birth, or a new beginning. The students went to Don Miguel one by one. They placed their hands on the stone wall, with one hand on either side of the waterfall. Don Miguel then guided their heads and upper bodies through the cold rushing water and back out in a form of a "baptism." After experiencing the water, the student would say in an authoritative voice, "I am alive!" For me, this was an invigorating experience on many levels.

# Tupananchiscama

f you remember from my meeting with the Q'ero, there is an expression, *tupananchiscama*, which means, "Until we meet again." This meaning includes meeting again on this level or on different levels of being. We much prefer this thought than that of goodbye, which indicates an ending. Being in the presence of Don Miguel, Gini, and their group had been very special for me. I was reluctant to separate from them. I said "tupananchiscama" to them and explained the meaning. It is rare that you meet a teacher, mentor, or colleague as extraordinary as Don Miguel. He is accomplished in both the modern scientific world and timeless spiritual world of the Toltec culture. Being in his company for these precious days convinced me that I could walk both paths in balance, harmony, and joy. As our world pushes the edges of the scientific with ever-increasing fast-paced technology, it is essential that we heed the ancient, timeless truths. This knowledge will add depth, meaning, and continuity to our lives.

With these thoughts, my sense of urgency to preserve and share the Inca traditions, culture, and beliefs increased. As I parted with Don Miguel, I consoled myself in the realization that this separation was only a beginning and that I would meet with him again, both physically and in alternate dimensions. Time would prove both of these realities to be true.

# THREE LAWS REVEALED

**W**ell before dawn, I left the hotel in the village of Aguas Calientes sitting at the base of the mountain. The buses, filled with tourists, would not begin their zigzag ascent up the side of the mountain to enter Machu Picchu for another two hours. There was one hotel at the top, but it was expensive. Most of the people on the tours actually preferred to stay in the village at the bottom. The village has many hotels, quaint restaurants, and interesting shops of native creations. At the top of the main street, on a steep incline with many steps, you can relax in the natural hot springs. This is the reason for the name of the village, Aguas Calientes, "Hot Springs." The people in the village welcome the tourists and are very hospitable. I have many friends in this cozy village. I had been coming here for many years. Each time I come to Aguas Calientes and Machu Picchu, I am more comfortable and more enticed by the power and mystery of the sacred place. I never see the trip as routine. Machu Picchu always excites me.

I could see my breath as I climbed the road in the dark. This was a morning of free time for my tour group and, therefore, for me. The group was compatible and interested in the Incan beliefs and traditions. They had politely listened to the official tour guides, who accompany the group upon entering the site. These guides offer a great deal of historical information at a number of the special locations in this ancient mystical city. Later, many people in the group had many questions for me about the metaphysical meanings of these same sights. We retraced some of our steps, and I told them some of the many Inca legends. The group had many questions about the meaning of the "Sacred City," where they were experiencing so much energy and power.

The inhabitants of this city are Light Beings. Each member of the group expressed their increasing excitement about returning tonight to explore the City and its mysteries at night. (Nighttime tours of the Sacred City are not available any longer.) I liked this group because they asked interesting questions. Even as I answered their questions, I could hear myself unfolding. It was important to me to be able to express the richness of the power of the Inca Way. So here I was, climbing up in the dark so that I could be at the site at dawn. Perhaps Inti, the Sun, would enlighten me with the first light. I felt a sense of urgency to reach a small cave in Machu Picchu, where I wanted to meditate on the most important aspects of the Inca beliefs, the Inca Laws. I walked faster to reach the entrance to the city. My only companions on the road were a multitude of stars and the full moon on this crisp, clear pre-dawn. Like the puma, I needed to walk alone to satisfy my hunger, the quest for deeper meaning of these laws in the everyday experience of my life.

# Arms of Pachamama

A rriving at Machu Picchu in the darkness is truly "awesome." Seeing the ancient temples peek out from the shadows of the moonlight gives them a mystical glow that is lost in the brightness of the day. Being a tour guide, I knew most of the guards for many years and had no problem gaining entrance at this early hour. The quiet and solitude were comforting as I approached the first ancient gate to the City. I stopped, as usual, and asked for permission to enter from the Apus and the Guardian Spirits of the Sacred Site. My heart was filled with gratitude to the spirits for allowing me to visit their City. It always felt like a privilege to "be invited." It was in 1911 that these great Spirits allowed the Sacred City to be re-opened. I will always be grateful to Hiram Bingham, not only for his discovery, but also for spreading the word of the importance of this place to the entire world. All of the Children of the Sun, everyone on the entire planet, are welcomed back to this special place that, fortunately, had escaped total destruction. I was also grateful to the government for all of their careful restorations that truly enhanced the majesty of the site without destroying the integrity of the ancient city. This is a place of Power and Light. It is not a "ruin." It is very much alive.

Never was this belief more tangible to me than on this early morning in the moonlight. At every turn I could feel the presence of the life force on different levels of the Pacha. It took me less than ten minutes to walk to my first destination. I walked down the steps for about three or four meters, turned left, and entered a small cave that is overlooked by most people. The cave of granite, with veins of white quartz, is nearly four meters in depth and seven meters wide. The roof of the cave slopes dramatically from two-and-a-half meters, diminishing in height toward a rock wall in its interior. It is quite inviting and comfortable to sit and meditate with your back to the granite wall. You are able to look out above the Urubamba River to the facing mountain known as Yanantin. Most importantly, it is one of the places that is illuminated with the first light of the sunrise in Machu Picchu.

The air smelled fresh and earthy as I arrived at the cave. The finches, swallows, and sparrows were the first to notice the coming dawn and signaled me with their morning song. I quickly settled myself and entered a deep meditation, connecting almost instantly with Tayta Inti (inner Sun) and with Hatun Inti (the great central Sun), which is the manifestation of the Creator.

# Connecting to the Three Worlds

The rays of the sun were just breaking over the peaks of the distant mountains as I ended my meditation. I decided that I would next connect to the three Worlds: Uku Pacha, Kay Pacha, and Hanan Pacha. I climbed the steps and walked a short distance to a place that has three levels. A visitor has to lower his or her head, as if bowing in reverence, to enter a subterranean room with only one tiny window. One can almost feel the snake's presence in the dampness of the floor. The mind is quick to focus on the heavy energies, especially the emotions of fear and self-doubt. My inventory of sorrows and regrets are all too ready to slither into my consciousness as I am swallowed into my inner Lower World. Once I reached this inner space, I intentionally spun my internal energies from left to right in order to balance the masculine and feminine forces within me. I was now connected with all of my energy. Facing all of my heavy energies and putting them into kintuis, I then threw them to the ground, asking the Mother to transmute them.

I then proceeded from the darkness into the sunlight, as the Mother Earth re-birthed me into the Middle World of this reality. I was now basking in the beauty of the early sunlight. I climbed up the few steps and walked out to the balcony from which you can drink in the beauty of creation. A smile came to my lips, as I felt so grateful to the sun. I welcomed Inti with my opened arms. I could feel with my hands the presence and connection to Wayna Picchu on my left and Machu Picchu on my right. The Apus of these two great mountains were supporting me. I stood there with outstretched arms with the palms of my hands seeming to touch the two mountains. Yes, I could feel the presence of the mountains through my hands. Immediately, with open arms, I remembered that the heart opens with the spreading of your arms and the happiness of Putu Cusi comes to you and stays with you forever. We claim our connection to the cosmos as we open our arms and hearts to our family and friends. At these moments, the joy of Being is stirred in our hearts. It is a way to connect to higher levels of consciousness.

# Becoming the Inca

ollowing my experience of joy in connecting with the three worlds, I decided to return to the cave and sit for a while. The sun was warming, and I became very relaxed. After some time, I was in an altered state. I wasn't asleep but I felt myself start to walk around the city. The buildings looked different, a little brighter. I wasn't surprised since the sky was getting brighter as well. I then turned the corner near the Temple of the Condor and entered the dream. I was still walking, now in the Temple, but I was no longer alone. More and more people were gathering. The city was "coming alive." I wasn't sure if I was asleep and dreaming or if suddenly many people had arrived at Machu Picchu.

The next second, I was aware of unfamiliar sounds of words that I was hearing and noticed that the people were dressed in distinctive clothing. I was in Machu Picchu, but in the Machu Picchu of my ancestors, the ancient Incas. The term, Children of the Sun, took on new meaning as I looked into their faces. Their eyes were so "clear" and intense. As they acknowledged each other, every muscle in their face formed a smile and a warm greeting. I found it strange to observe such openness and mutual affection between the people. Their happiness seemed genuine with a sense of shared well-being. The good will was contagious. Suddenly, someone asked me if I had eaten breakfast. Recovering from my shock of being noticed, I said, "No I haven't!" If my language seemed strange to her, this lovely elderly lady gave no indication of it. She gestured that I should take a seat next to her in the small courtyard. I accepted her invitation, my confidence growing with each moment. The lady offered me some coca leaves. As is our tradition, I accepted the coca leaves with two hands out of respect for the spirit of the Mama Coca. I quickly grabbed my bag of coca leaves to reciprocate her gesture of friendship.

# Munay

My first inquiry to my benefactor, as we ate our bread and cheese, was how long she had lived in Machu Picchu. "I have lived here all my life. I was born here and have never wanted to be anywhere else," was her reply. She continued, "Some of my brothers have left for other cities, but they return when they can. Everyone loves to be here where the Inti is hitched to Pachamama." "It is very beautiful here. I have heard of the Hitching Post of the Sun," I said, wanting to expand the conversation. "Is that why everyone here appears to be so happy, so full of light?" The lady responded, "The people here don't just have the appearance of happiness, they live their happiness. They live in the love that the Father Sun has for Mother Earth. As Incas, Children of the Sun, we spend our days reflecting the Father's love by honoring and caring for all of the creation that we experience living in harmony with Pachamama.

"The Mother and all of creation cares for us, providing all that we need to live, such as food and clothing. We reciprocate by caring for the creation in love and gratitude. As Children of the Sun, we share in and reflect the love of Inti for the Pachamama and the Mother for the Father. We are all one in the Divine Pacha's consciousness of love that we call '*tucuy munayniyoc.*' We live in this state here in Machu Picchu and share in the joy and abundance of the Pacha. When your heart is full of the joy and love of the Cosmos, it leaves no room for troubling energies. Truth and love are essential to the Inca way of life. Speak the truth and act with love and you nurture the Divine spark within you.

"This is what you see in the faces of the people. This is the normal state of being of the Incas. The people here are so full of the love (Munay) that you will see the Cosmos send a message announcing the state of tucuy munayniyoc. As a cosmic messenger, the hummingbird flies over the heads of the Children of the Sun, trying to sip the nectar of the Children's expanded love." Saying all of this, the lady offered me more coca leaves. I was busy looking at the beautiful expressions on the faces of the people and scanning for the hummingbirds. I thought about asking the lady her name, but I didn't want to be presumptuous and waited for her to ask me mine first.

# Llancay

A s I chewed the coca leaves, my mind filled with questions. I wanted to be respectful, but I also wanted to know more about the life of the people. I had been watching many inhabitants carrying bundles and others sweeping and performing the usual tasks of daily life. Fearing that the lady would leave, I got up the nerve to ask another question. "How do you divide up the work and the responsibilities in taking care of Pachamama with the crops and animals?" The lady looked at me for a long period of time as if to read my thoughts. I felt a familiar discomfort like I did when talking with the mysterious lady of my youth. She must have sensed my distress because she broke into a smile and said, "Oh you want to know about how people work and organize things." "Yes," I said, "if you don't mind talking further." She replied, "I don't mind, but I would prefer to walk now and take you to my home." I smiled internally at my memories of another walk with a lady.

After a short way, the lady said, "When you live here in the presence of the love, work is experienced as ultimate service to the Divine. It is a privilege to have this experience. Llancay is the opportunity in this reality to imitate the care of the Divine for all of creation. To perform any service for another person, the animals, the plants, the stones, is a work of love for the Mother. Work is never a punishment. It is an opportunity to express your unique gift with everyone and everything. You express your power through your service to yourself, your family and the community. This is what you are experiencing in Machu Picchu.

"The father has planted the seed of love in our hearts, and Llancay is our expression of that love of the creation. We are all one in the expression of the love and joy of the Divine Essence, the Pacha. Love and service are different expressions of the light sent from the Divine through Father Sun, Inti, to every level of being on Mother Earth. We call this 'tucuy llancayniyoc.' It is in this state of consciousness that we manifest, or co-create, the abundance of love from the Cosmos into this world of experience. In love and services, the Inca can enter into many levels of consciousness with unlimited resources. Machu Picchu is one manifestation of this abundance. It is a special place that has special power and energy that can assist you in going to higher levels of consciousness because the people here live in love and service. The power of this place comes from their love and service in connection to the Divine."

We had arrived at the lady's house. I was now feeling strangely comfortable as ideas that I had tried to understand from the elders in the Paratia and Q'ero communities were coming alive in the present.

# Yachay

The lady's house was built of stone like most of the houses in Machu Picchu. It was located near the Temple of the Sun. Along our path, we paused to drink the fresh mountain water from the Sacred Fountains. Other memories returned of the walk I took with the mysterious lady so many years ago. At age eleven, I didn't want to know anything about the Incas, let alone their laws. Now, at age thirty-eight, I wanted to know it all. It had been an interesting journey since I last thought of the lady and our walk to my house through the stream so many years before.

Lost in my memories, I was a bit startled when this lady of Machu Picchu said, "Wipe your feet before you come in." I went into the tidy room and sat on a small seat carved into the wall near the opening of the door. The lady sat opposite me. "I think you are very close to experiencing your authentic self." I was very confused by this statement. How did this lady know anything about me? I didn't have much time to question her proclamation as she continued, "The real beginning of knowing the third part of how an Inca lives is to know your authentic self. You can only do this by paying attention to the energies inside of you. It is necessary to nurture both the polarities of the masculine and the feminine within yourself. When you can recognize your inner authentic self, you can begin to balance the powerful polarities.

"At the moment of balancing the energies through love and service in the world of experience, you can spiral upward toward the sun and explode into the consciousness of the Pacha, the Divine. Then all is one, and you can know from deep inside your being at all levels of consciousness, or realities. This is called 'tucuy yachayniyoc.' This state does not come from the intellect of the conscious mind. It is the understanding of the Mother Earth in relation to the Cosmos that blossoms into wisdom. Wisdom is experienced and known with the heart, rather than known with the mind. Wisdom comes from the connection to the knowing of your inner spirit self that is directly connected to the Pacha. You become one with the wisdom of the Cosmos."

After taking a long breath, the lady continued, "Once this explosion occurs, inner awareness bursts forth with wisdom. You live in such harmony with the Pacha that you understand the wisdom of the Inca, the joy of being." There seemed to be an explosion of light in the small room. The lady stood as she said, "You are now born into the life of the Inca, a Child of the Sun, who is equally at home in his heart and in all the Cosmos." The priestess reached out and touched my heart saying, "Welcome home, Child of the Sun." I instantly felt a part of the cosmic family and one with all of creation.

# High Priest

felt a strong hand on my shoulder. I looked up, covering my eyes from the radiance of the light in the room. A formidable, yet not threatening, Inca stood in the doorway, with his hand on my shoulder. I recognized immediately that this was an *illac umo*, one who radiates light. An aura of light was coming from his head and his steady gaze was entrancing. I felt a state of reverence and intense curiosity as to why such a radiant being was taking time to be here with me. After a moment, he smiled and spoke, "Come, Inca, and walk with me." As I emerged from the house, I could not see for a few seconds until my eyes adjusted to the overwhelming light. Not only was it a sunny day, this tall Inca intensified the effect of the sun. The Inca started off in a deliberate manner. I followed him to an area where we could work with our energy and resonance within different vibrational realities. We went into the room behind the main temple. I knew this place well and had brought many groups here. You can say a few words rather softly and they quickly travel around the perimeter of the outdoor room in echoes. This place is between the main plaza and the hitching post.

The Inca intoned a sound. It wasn't 'ohm' but was similar. He intoned 'kon' on three different tonal levels. I could feel the vibration of my body respond differently to each intonation. He then gestured for me to imitate the ritual. My first try was rather good in my opinion as I intoned 'kon' on three levels. My teacher only smiled. He then placed my hand on his diaphragm to experience how it puffed outward as he repeated the ritual. When he was finished, I was conscious of every part of my body as I tried to imitate his movements. I took in a deep breath and tried to puff my diaphragm as

I intoned the 'kon,' As my body vibrated in sound, I was immediately in a transcendental state of oneness with the Divine. By the end of the third 'kon' I realized that I was tearing with joy. I had never experienced such a state of bliss, being wanted, being safe, being planned for from all time, being loved, and being an individual within the oneness of all creation.

In a few moments, the High Priest said, "Now you are ready to go to the top of the pyramid." This is the place in Machu Picchu that we call the Hitching Post of the Sun. Actually, it is the top point of the pyramid that connects with the pyramid in the Cosmos. We can also say it connects the Spiral of the Mother Earth with the Spiral of the Cosmos. This is the space of now, the present, the gift. Every moment is a gift of the Cosmos. It is the gift to be! You are the center of the four directions with 'kon' above, and 'tiki' below ('kon,' the Comic Gatherer energy and 'tiki,' the Cosmic Mother Energy).

The Priest invited me to go up to the monolith, kneel, and place my third eye on the ancient sacred stone. Immediately, my third eye "opened." I was looking into the Cosmos. The veils dropped, and I could "see" into different realities that are present in the multitude of layers of pyramids that were suddenly present in my consciousness. It was an explosion of being infinite and eternal. The emotions were of total integration and limitless expansion. This is an entire body sensation, and you immediately realize that you have more than five senses. Your mind is engaged. Your emotions are engaged. Your body is engaged. You glimpse your being beyond the reality of the physical, but including the physical. In this state, colors have a texture and a tactile experience. The color has a vibration, and you experience more subtlety of tone. Not being a musician, I can't fully express this experience. The Inca then said to me, "My child, realize that the power is not in the stone. The power is innate in you. This is a place that connects the energies that re-ignite your own inner spark of light. It is a place of re-awakening. You have all within. There are the seeds of Munay, Llancay, Yachay in your heart. Activate them three times three. Remember and awaken to be who you are, an Inca, a Child of the Sun."

The Inca then turned abruptly and started to walk down toward what is called the Temple of the Condor. Knowing that the condor lives between this reality and other realities, I was anxious to hear what the Inca would say. As we arrived, he commented that, "The condor doesn't kill, but transmutes food. The condor flies in different dimensions, but soars in this reality."

The Inca explained, "There is a hole in the stone beak of the condor in Machu Picchu to take messages to Pachamama and the Lower World. This condor always remains in the east in the sunrise. The condor can teach you to fly. You will see that your life and everything you are doing is perfect, in that it is useful for your journey to the Cosmos. As you soar, you can see your life in the past and in the future." He continued, "Your past is your future as your future is your past. It is necessary to remember from your past in the present to see how you hold on to your favorite heavy energy. This would be the one that helps you to live in fear. It is fear that binds you and doesn't allow you to soar. Only you can un-tether your own spirit. Leave your fear with the condor to transmute, and then we can go, and your spirit can soar with the joy of being alive."

I touched the rising stone wings, remembering that "our wings" are in balance when we connect with our own energy. I remembered my fears and asked the condor to transmute the energy of the fear into openness and acceptance. Heavy forces, such as fear and regret, block our inner spiritual flow. We need to be respectful of their presence overshadowing our innate power and wait for the special moment when we can bypass their power and soar.

# Testing the Fear

The Inca said, "Now we will test how well you have released the fear so you can soar." Apprehension was mixed with excitement as I walked with the High Priest to the "funeral rock." All the area around the funeral rock is like a large apacheta. In performing an apacheta, we had to cleanse ourselves of our heavy energy before we got to the Crystal City, the mystical Machu Picchu. According to one famous yatiri, funeral rock is the stone where we can journey to the west to face fear, our remorseful feelings, our judgments, even to face death. After this releasing process, we can claim from the east new light bodies as authentic Children of the Sun.

I laid on the funeral rock on my back and opened my arms slightly at my side with my head facing west. This place is a transportation tool to the other dimensions. I waited until my mind, spirit, and body were ready to face and release my fear. All of a sudden, I was engulfed in sadness and anger. The emotions came in waves. With the help and strength of the Inca and with the support of the surrounding Apus, the fear and anger subsided. I was empty. My arms seemed to open wide on their own volition, with no effort. From the East came a rush of emotion. I felt solid and strong. My body was light; it seemed that I could levitate off the rock and off the mountain. Suddenly, I was soaring in a state of confidence as I claimed a new light body. I was in communion with this place and with the Cosmos. I had awakened.

A different knowing, a new wisdom, filled my physical body, my conscious mind and my authentic spiritual self. I experienced more this way than through my senses and my thoughts, I experienced spirit, my spirit. Fountains of love and creativity were flowing within me. I was experiencing the joy of being. This state of being extended far beyond the limitations of my senses or my thoughts. I felt forever connected to the Divine and all that is. The Inca said, "Always remember this moment of reclaiming your heritage. When you see the rainbow, acknowledge that you are an embodied Light Being, an individual ray of Hatun Inti, the Sun behind the sun."

# Back in the Moment

"Jorge, Jorge Luis, how are you?" I blinked my eyes a few times and focused on the person calling my name. This was not an Inca High Priest. It was Ciro, a friend and fellow tour guide. His smiling face took me by surprise and I tried to re-capture the face of the Inca. I looked around to see many tourists, not residents of Machu Picchu, scurrying in all directions. Reluctantly I had to leave the ancient reality and rejoin the present moment in time. My friend's face quickly had turned to one of concern. "Jorge Luis, are you okay?" Ciro repeated his concerned question. "Yes, yes I am wonderful," was my immediate reply. "I just had the most interesting experience," I continued with much enthusiasm. Now I could see that my friend was getting even more worried about me as he took a step back and curiously studied my face. I laughed and said, "Really, I am fine. Do you have time to have some lunch with me?" Ciro relaxed a bit and replied, "I have almost two hours before I am expected to return to my group again. Let's go eat. You must need food because you are acting a little strange." Again I laughed as I gathered my backpack and jacket and we walked toward the restaurant at the top of Machu Picchu near to the hotel. We ordered our food at the cafeteria side of the restaurant and found a table outside where we could talk uninterrupted.

Ciro listened intently as I told him about my meditation that ushered me into my walk with the Priestess and High Priest of ancient Machu Picchu. "Remember how we were taught in school that the Inca Laws were: Don't lie, don't steal, don't be lazy?" I asked. "Of course, everybody learned the Laws," was his reply as he shrugged his shoulders. "You know that I have been interviewing and working with the paq'os and yatiris for awhile now," I said. "Sure, ever since the work with the BBC a few year ago," Ciro answered as he ate his soup and reached for the bread. "Exactly," I continued, "the Q'ero have told me that these were not the Inca Laws of our ancestors. They said that the ancient Inca Laws were: Munay - Love, Llancay - Work or Service, and Yachay – Wisdom. They also told me that through these natural Laws you could learn to live in accordance with the Cosmos and raise your level of consciousness. But I never fully understood the meaning of these Laws and how one could use them to live the Inca path. So I came here early this morning to meditate and think about the Laws. During the meditation I had a mystical experience and had the Incas of long ago make their Laws clear to me in my mind." Again Ciro was looking at me with a face full of concern and question. "Is that why you were acting so strangely when I first saw you?" was his remark. Laughingly, I replied, "Of course, your hand on my shoulder was what ended the meditation." Ciro again relaxed and then got a serious look on his face. "Tell me more of what you learned about the Incas," he asked as we cleared the table.

We started to walk toward the mountain of Machu Picchu off the path where we found a spot to sit and talk further with the ancient city below us. I was thinking about my mystical experience and all that was revealed from my heart to my mind. This was the real test, presented to me so quickly this afternoon. Could I really be a useful cacharuna and interpret what I learned to Ciro and even the people in my tour group, who were so interested in the Inca beliefs? I decided that telling Ciro about the Laws could be even more difficult than telling strangers who had not grown up with the teachings in our schools about the Incas. This was important to me so I welcomed Ciro's interest and hoped that I could satisfy his curiosity with my newly revealed information.

I took a long deep breath and began to explain. "Munay is the flowing of the natural love of the Cosmos for all things. This love is for all of creation. We have an inner spring of love that is natural to us. It just flows. Love is the expression of God in your being. When you love another being you treat them with care and respect. You appreciate them. You are not quick to anger and seek revenge when you truly love someone or something. You keep your self-respect, but you always try to extend the love you feel from the Divine to all other things. You do this for all of the people in your daily life, the good ones, and the not-so-good ones. If you are coming from a place of love, you live life as much as you can in truth and avoid lies. This action is difficult because not everybody will treat you with love and respect. You do not have to act like them in return. You can live everyday in truth and with respect. You also need to respect what belongs to others and not take from others what is theirs. This refers to their belongings, their dignity, and their feelings. You respect a person by avoiding interference with their loved ones of their ability to make a decent living. You treat everyone and everything like a brother or sister as an expression of Divine Love."

Ciro looked at me intensely, saying, "If everyone lived like that, it would be a peaceful place to live, but many people only look out for themselves and do not care about the well-being of others." I replied, "This is true, but we are called to change this by living like true Incas, The Children of the Sun. It is a challenge, but each one of us can effect change if *we* change." Ciro shrugged, "Well this is true but not always easy. I guess this would cover 'don't lie and don't steal'." I was encouraged by his interest and replied, "Yes, of course, it is true that you should not lie or steal, but did you notice that the true Inca Laws are positive, not negative? Human laws are made with the mind out of fear. The Inca Laws come from the Divine Love of the Cosmos. The energy is positive, and, if practiced, the Laws have another purpose: to raise your level of consciousness and live in *sonccoqui*, the joy and abundance of the Cosmos. There is a very different energy vibration in loving rather than in what not to do. The ancient Incas were positive, uplifting people."

"If Llancay is about work, then is that the positive of 'don't be lazy'?" Ciro questioned. "Well, yes and no, for it is much more that this," was my reply. "Work for the Inca was a blessing. It was an expression of interacting with and taking care of the creation. Llancay, it is work, but not as a punishment. Work is a great opportunity to give a hand to the Mother Earth to bring abundance and prosperity to everybody. They see work as an opportunity for the expression of the essence and purpose of each person, each animal, each plant, each rock, and each spirit. It is how each individual expresses himself or herself in this reality. Llancay is about creativity without limits. All work can be seen as interacting with all creation in a positive way. All honest work is a welcomed expression of a person's talent or good will.

"This is what *ayni*, or reciprocity, is about. Reciprocity is basically mutual care and respect in all interactions between people or nature. Whatever we do for the Mother repays her care for us — the food, the shelter, and all the blessings she gives us. It is the same with people, animals, and even things. We need to care for them if they are going to be there for us."

Ciro was pensive as he thought about what I had said. "Okay," he finally said, "I can see how work can be seen as something valuable. I certainly love my job, and I would be bored if I had nothing to do, but some people really have too much work and too little to eat. How does that fit into this Law?" I was excited that my friend was listening with such interest and welcomed his challenge. I responded, "You are right in that not all people get enough from their efforts or work. You are really helping me think this through my friend! There is another meaning of Llancay, which is service. Every Inca, every Child of the Sun, also has the gift of service in that he or she can assist their fellow man in some way. So if one man helps another to learn a trade, or provides meaningful work for that person, this man helps the community.

"As you know, the Inca tradition everywhere, even today, places a lot of meaning on family and care of the extended family." "Yes, of course, family has always been very important to the people," Ciro agreed. Having his undivided attention, I went on, "Well, this service is the extension of this care to the entire community of the region and then to all of mankind. When you put extra effort into service for the greater good of the people, you have power, and you are following the Inca Law of Llancay." "What do you mean by power?" asked Ciro. My reply was instant, "When you live in love and service for others in the community, you have the power to change circumstances for the better for everybody in this physical reality, and you attain a higher consciousness in the world of the Spirits."

"It's true, if everyone lived this way, it would be very pleasant," Ciro commented. After thinking for a moment, he continued, "Do you think that life in Machu Picchu in ancient times was lived in this kind of love and service?" I replied, "Yes! That was what I was experiencing in my mystical experience. Everyone was living in harmony. You can see why I didn't want to leave this experience." Ciro laughed and pointed his finger at me, as he seemed to recall how startled and reluctant I appeared when he first called out to me. "I think that you were having a very good time in ancient Machu Picchu my friend," was his only comment as he stood up to leave. I was ready to continue, but Ciro had to meet his group, so our conversation about the Inca Laws ended. Yachay would have to wait for another time.

# Seeking Wisdom

ime had been distorted for me since I arrived at Machu Picchu this morning. I hadn't realized that we had spent over an hour and a half together. I walked to the main entrance, thinking about all of the experiences of the day. The crowd of tourists quickly enveloped me as I waited for a bus ride down the mountain to the village. The ride down the mountain is always filled with laughter as one of the local boys gets on the bus to say goodbye to the tourists. He then gets off the bus and follows a straight-line path down the mountain side as the tourist bus winds its way toward the village. As the road zigzags back and forth across the mountainside, this young boy, about age twelve, jumps on to the road just prior to the bus passing the path, and then calls out "goodbye" to the passing tourists at each leg of the trip back to Aguas Calientes. At each shout of "goodbye" from the youth, the passengers wave and laugh in response. After many encounters between the boy and tourists, the bus stops and the boy climbs aboard to complete the journey. Collecting his hard-earned tips along the way, this young entrepreneur never departs empty-handed.

When I arrived in the village of Aguas Calientes, I decided to take a walk to visit my friend, Marco, who has a small shop on the main street. Marco makes beautiful jewelry, and I wanted to invite him to meet my tour group after dinner to show the group samples of his creations. In the vicinity of Machu Picchu, there are two stones that the local people cut, polish, and artistically craft into beautiful jewelry. One stone is called serpentine and is dark green with white veins through it. Many craftsmen design the serpentine stone into an Inca Cross, an open circle surrounded with the three steps of the Three Worlds on each of the four sides. The Inca Crosses are very beautiful and popular with tourists. The second stone is similar to an opal, with a light green and gray combination of colors. Besides jewelry, these two stones and several other lesser-known stones are used to carve symbolic animals for ceremonies. These beautiful carved stones and crystals are used on home mesas or as mementos of Machu Picchu, or Peru.

I walked into Marco's shop and looked at his latest creations while he tended to a customer. After a few moments, he was free, so we moved to the back room of his shop. We exchanged greetings, and I invited him to come to the hotel with samples of his work. Marco wanted to keep his shop open late that evening, so his wife agreed to join my tour group with the samples at the hotel, instead. Marco requested that I stay for a while and join him in cups of coca tea at the café next door. I readily accepted his hospitality.

After a few minutes of conversation, Marco surprised me when he asked, "What is going on with you today?" "What do you mean?" I replied. "Well, you seem distracted and only half here, like you have something on your mind," he answered. "You are very observant my friend," I said laughingly. Of course, I had been thinking about all that had happened that day, but I did not think that it was noticeable to others. I guess that I am not a good pretender and my friends know me very well. I proceeded to recount to Marco the day's events. He listened attentively, making no comment.

When I finished my explanation about the Priestess and High Priest, Marco looked at me intensely, saying, "I understand the meaning of Munay as Love and Llancay as Work or Service, but I don't understand Yachay or Wisdom." He went on, "How do you experience the 'authentic self' and how do you experience wisdom?" I was surprised that Marco was so interested in the messages of my mystical experience. Since he had listened to me without comment, I assumed he was just being polite as a good friend. Of course, I was thrilled that he had such insight and interest.

As I explained the message of the true meaning of the Inca Laws, I understood them more, not only with my mind, but also in my heart. It seemed like the Priestess implanted a seed of truth in me that was growing each time I related the Laws to another. I remembered that the Inca Laws had been presented to me by many paqo's and yatiris in the highlands. They told me that if I meditated on the Laws that the Laws would have increasing clarity. I felt that if I could instill this information, the awareness of the true meaning of the Inca Laws, to Marco that in time their meaning would become real and useful in his life.

Marco was waiting for an answer regarding the Law of Wisdom. I thought for a moment while I asked for more tea. Finally, I said, "Well, we can stay locked in our personalities and habits, or we can take the time to be aware that there is a self, a higher spirit, or a soul that lies deep within us. This is our authentic self that is our spiritual self that lives beyond the physical body and beyond the conscious mind. It experiences many levels of reality, yet it is always with us and accessible right here and right now.

"Physically we are either male or female, but inside we have both attributes in a unique and individual way. We also have within us both heavy and refined energies. You know that we try to give the heavy energies, the sorrow, regret, and the guilt to Pachamama in our ceremonies. We do this to have Mother Earth transmute these energies into lighter energy and remove the heaviness from our heart. Love, service, meditation, and ceremony can all help the refined energies grow in our heart and in our conscious awareness. This is living life with intention and purpose.

"You will become more aware that you are a spiritual being, as well as a physical and thinking being. As you pay attention to your inner urges and feelings, they will come to you more readily. Some people call this intuition. But if you refine your intuition to inner knowing with the love of Munay and the service of Llancay, you will experience the wisdom of Yachay. This inner knowing from the authentic self will take you to higher levels of consciousness within yourself and within all Creation. There is a sense of inner peace and joy regardless of what events are occurring in your life. You are then living in the experience of Yachay as you live in harmony and unity with the Cosmos. You are living with greater awareness. You are living with the freedom to experience the joy of being at any moment. "

After a while, Marco replied, "You have given me a great deal to think about. I have not heard the higher consciousness explained in this way before. You have said a lot in this brief time, and I thank you for these insights. I hope we can talk again after I have had time to digest this new awareness. I truly appreciate your telling me of your experience. I could have such a conversation with only a few people. Again, I thank you my friend." I was touched by Marco's words and decided that it was important for me to tell others of my experience. Everyone could then have the opportunity to listen or not, or to listen as they were ready to hear.

I finished my tea and walked down the many steps towards my hotel room. I needed to shower and eat before I met my tour group for our evening at Machu Picchu. Anticipating my return to Machu Picchu, I wondered if my mystical experience would continue that night. The weather was clear, so the stars would be magnificent. I felt confident that the group would have many wonderful experiences visiting the ancient city tonight.

# Endings and Beginnings

We had many interesting ceremonies that evening, but I did not meet any other ancient Inca Priest or Priestess. I did tell the tour group from the United States about my mystical experience as we visited the many Sacred Sites that I encountered earlier in my morning meditation. The group was reverent and curious about my metaphysical tale. Eventually, one fellow, Theron, asked, "How can we use these laws in our everyday life. Too often I hear things that sound awesome, but after I get back to my routine I lose the impact and enthusiasm of the message." "This is a very important point," I answered. "Let me think for a moment and together, maybe we can answer this problem." After a short time I said, "The first Inca Law, Munay, is really the foundation. It is, basically, an attitude of acceptance and appreciation towards your fellow man, as well as the Cosmos. Focus on the positive, and avoid holding on to anger and resentment. For example, I don't drive a car, but often I see people here in Peru, and even more so in your country, driving and angry at the other drivers. Some people, in general, are gracious and co-operative. Some people, on the other hand, are not so nice or co-operative.

"It is important to live in the understanding that people think differently and will often behave in ways we don't agree with or understand. Yes, it is necessary to seek truth and speak the truth, but, very often, people have different ideas of what is true and just. It is important to realize that not everyone thinks in the same way or is at the same point in seeking the Divine. Do what you can to remedy or ease any situation that you feel is unjust, but do not live in a sate of retaliation. Holding on to heavy, angry emotions robs you of your joy and your ability to progress to higher levels of expanded consciousness."

"That can be a challenge for anyone living in our fast and busy world, let alone someone who has suffered at the hands of others," was the quick reply from Alicia, one woman in the group. "Yes, it is certainly more of a challenge for some, but it is important for all. Sometimes the people who suffer the most are the first to forgive, though," I said softly, and continued, "The greatest challenge may be to not hate someone who has caused harm to someone you love. It may be natural to be angry and to take appropriate action, but to live with hate while seeking retaliation solves nothing. For many of us, it seems even harder to change the habit of being angry about daily slights than major events. We honor ourselves when we live in truth and with a positive, caring attitude toward all people and all of nature."

"But what about all the injustices in life?" asked another voice. "This is where the second Law, Llancay builds on the first law," I replied. I was surprised that the group at this late hour was so interested in the Inca Laws. This curiosity energized me, so I continued. "If we are productive in some way in society and express the attitude of love or caring in our hearts, we perform a service to others and to the Cosmos. Whatever you choose to do – have a career, a job, or work in the home – you can perform service. If you perform your chosen work with a conscious attitude of good will, honesty, and respect for the environment, you are enriching your life and the lives of others. You are living consciously and with the correct attitude.

If you see injustice, then you can work toward a solution. Some problems are very complicated, but right-minded people, who work in the spirit of Munay, love or caring, will find solutions. This law, Llancay is for everyone in every occupation. But you do not have to work all the time!" I added with a laugh. "In some cases, you can do as much service spending time listening to a friend as you can working all the day."

After a few laughs and a brief pause, Theron said, "Thank you. They are wonderful insights, but what about the third law, Yachay? How do I practice Yachay?" I thought for a moment, and replied, "I suggest that you take a few moments in the morning and in the evening to quiet the busyness of your mind. Think of your worries, or heavy energies, and give them to Pachamama, or a Light Being of your tradition, for transformation and healing. Spend a few moments offering thanks for all of the blessings you receive from the Divine and from others. You can do this in meditation, in prayer, or in motion. I suggest that every morning you start your day facing east, preferably outdoors, and greet the Inti with open arms in thanksgiving for the opportunity of a new day. Open your arms to drink in the light and the love. Take your right hand and place it on your heart, saying in your mind, 'with love.' Then take your left hand and place on your solar plexus, saying 'without fear.'

"Taking a few moments to be aware and conscious will help you connect to the authentic self. Do this practice each day and make a special intention for the day. It is the little things that you do everyday that can have the most life-changing impact. After a little practice, you might find that, like with me, the Divine will offer many insights and gifts to you in response to your intentions. A knowing serenity will spring from deep within your heart to expand and balance the voice of your conscious mind."

"But what if the sun isn't shining or I can't get outside?" asked Alicia. "You can do this practice anywhere, anytime, and in any condition because the sun is always there," I replied. "It is always best to face east to where the sun rises, but that is all you need."

It was now past midnight, and I had been up since before dawn. All of the energy I had collected that day was melting away. I was eager to leave the Crystal City and get some sleep. Just as I turned to leave, Alicia asked me how the Inca Laws fit into PachaKuti. As I thought about this question, I got a small burst of energy. Without really thinking, I replied, "PachaKuti, as you know, is the beginning of a new cycle for mankind. In the PachaKuti, the coming of the Inca signals the expansion of the Christ Consciousness in the Christian tradition. This rise in consciousness allows our hearts to further open, bringing us into communion with the Christ Vibration. This Divine

Vibration Level attunes all the vibration levels of spirit, mind, and body of those people of all traditions seeking the Light. This Divine intervention allows us to become in harmony with all humanity, all of creation, all of the Light Being, and with Hatun Inti, the Sun behind the Sun, the Divine Essence. We are all very fortunate to be alive at this time and to be invited to be Incas, Children of the Sun. Our origin is in the Light, and we are destined to return to the Light." With this message in our thoughts, we left Machu Picchu.

One couple, in particular, was very desirous of returning to Peru to learn more about the Inca traditions and beliefs. They had many unanswered questions that evening as we departed Machu Picchu. In silence, we boarded the bus to return to the hotel. The following day, as we were returning to Cusco on the train, this curious couple asked about my journey in becoming a cacharuna. I smiled and remarked that I had never thought much about the topic. I told them that I had not intended to be involved with the metaphysical and had avoided it in my youth. The couple wanted to know more; however, the train was pulling into the station, and there was no time for further conversation. One day, I will ponder the unfolding of my spiritual quest, but not today. Today, I am going to rest and reflect on all that had happened while I was visiting the Crystal City, Machu Picchu.

# Epilogue

n the many years since I embraced the spiritual path of the chacaruna, I have not lost my love of science and technology. The gifts from our mind are both necessary and wonderful. Claiming our own authentic self and our spiritual heritage is not in contradiction to the scientific mind. It adds enrichment to our experience as human beings. As Children of the Sun, we are more than what we think and what we perceive through the five senses. Our spirit, our authentic self, is part of us. It is natural, that is all.

We do not have to study to find it, or be initiated, or search for it. It is in us. It is what gives you the energy of life. To connect to your spiritual self, you only need to remove the fear and doubt that your mind whispers to you. The mind is accustomed to being in control and will always try to keep control. You don't have to fight with the mind, just relax and experience what is beyond the mind.

Although I personally welcome you to visit my mystical Peru, it is not necessary to travel far or change from your own tradition and spiritual heritage. The point is to connect to your own spiritual body everyday, wherever you are. You can take a moment in your home, in nature, or in a church, temple or mosque to connect with the Sun behind the sun. In this moment, you can experience your authentic self, your spiritual body.

When you connect to the spirit, your creativity flows and you will enjoy your life in a richer way. You can have the intent to live in love, service, and wisdom as you interact with your family and your community. Your relationships and work can have more meaning as you draw energy and ideas from your authentic self. Life becomes richer in every aspect as you view all situations from an expanded, cosmic point of view. The purpose of life becomes the celebration of life itself.

Thank you for reading about my journey on my own spiritual path. It is my hope that these words touched your spirit, as well as your mind, and will lead to many more "awakenings." What I have said here is only a little grain of information from the vast spiritual heritage of the Incas. There is much more to come from myself and from my brothers and sisters of the Andes.

The journey continues.

# IMPORTANT NOTE FROM JORGE LUIS DELGADO

*This book is based on actual events in my life and has nothing to do with the official version of the history of my country. Some of the places mentioned can be difficult to find and traveling to them precarious. I highly recommend that you travel with an experienced guide to the "non-tourist" locations. You can only visit the Q'ero on Ausangate Mountain with a special invitation.*

APUS

Akamari
Ausangate
Illampu
Lady of Illimani
Machu Picchu
Mama Simona
Pachatussan
Pitusiray
Putu Cusi
Salkantay
Sawasiray
Tunupa
Wakac Willka
Wayna Picchu
Yanantin

# GLOSSARY

**Apacheta**
Stone brought by the bearer and often placed on other apacheta stones to release heavy energy to Mother Earth. It translates as "take it away."

**Apu**
Light Being that exists within special mountains. These Spirits live in both the Middle and Upper Worlds and can intercede for humanity. They are also referred to as Apukunas.

**Aramu Muru**
Legendary Master Teacher who brought the Golden Disc from the ancient continent of Lemuria to the Andes in order to connect the people to the Divine Central Sun.

**ayni**
Reciprocity. It reflects the necessity of caring for all people and all of nature in return for the blessings and care we receive each day.

**callawayas**
Special healers from the region of Charazani in Bolivia. They are known for their great knowledge of the healing power of herbs and travel extensively to perform healings.

**chacana**
Often referred to as the Andean or Inca Cross. It is a design in nature or manmade that reflects the three worlds with a central disc representing the Divine Central Sun.

**chacaruna**
"Bridge person" who helps one cross from one state of consciousness to other states of consciousness or other realms.

**chakra**
Translates as a field with crops. Included in the understanding of one's chakra are the fields, the animals, the house, and the family.

**challa**
The throwing of wine to Pachamama in the direction of the sun during ceremonies.

**chicha**
Locally brewed corn beer. When a person has chicha to sell, they put a red flag on display outside of their house.

**chincanas**
Manmade tunnels, large enough for humans, that run underground throughout the Andes and some islands on Lake Titicaca.

## cholla (o)
Native clothing with a European influence that has been worn in the Andes since the failed rebellion from the Spanish.

## chullpa
Ancient burial or ceremonial tower made from large stones.

## conopas
Llamas, alpacas, or flowers carved from stone or crystal with a hole bored on top. They are used in ceremonies and kept as a protector of the home.

## cuyas
Healing stones that are placed on a person's body or placed in a cloth and passed through their energy field.

## despacho
Colorful ceremonial offering to Pachamama or the Apus. It is built in layers with many ingredients by a yatiri or paq'o and the celebrants, and either buried or burned when completed.

## Hatun Inti
One name for Divinity or God. It is the Divine Central Sun behind the sun.

## hucha
Heavy energies such as guilt, regret, sorrow, shame, etc.

## illas
Rectangular four- or five-inch alabaster stones carved in the form of a chakra, with crops, animals, houses, and people of the family.

## Inti
The shortened use of Tayta Inti, Father Sun.

## kantuta
Fuchsia-like red flower that is a sign of hospitality. It is often called the Inca flower.

## kawsay
The energy that permeated all of Creation on various vibrational levels.

## kintui
A triad of coca leaves in a fan-like design. During Inca ceremonies, you often blow your intentions onto these coca leaves and offer them to Pachamama or the Apus.

## kontiki
The "kon," Divine Energy, with the "tiki" Earth Energy.

## ley line
An earth energy line.

## Llancay
One of the Three Inca Laws. It is the law of service, work, and creative expression of your individual gifts.

## Mama Coca

The Spirit of the coca plant that gives us many uses and many blessings. She is the symbol of our spiritual food.

## Mama Killa

Our name for the Moon.

## Mama Ocllo

Wife of the first Inca Manco Capac

## Mama Sara

Name of the Spirit of the corn plant. She symbolizes our physical food.

## Manco Capac

Legendary name of the first Inca sent from the Divine Central Sun to help all people. "Inca," in fact, means leader. The name is derived from Mallcu, meaning "the leader who flies," and Capac, meaning "the one who has the power."

## mesa

Translates in Spanish as "table." In the Inca tradition the mesa is an altar for Inca ceremonies.

## Munay

First of the Three Inca Laws. It is the Law of love. Rather than only an emotion, love is seen as an attitude of respect and appreciation for everyone and everything.

## Pacha

A concept that includes space, time, quantity, other realities, the Divinity, and what is still a mystery. It can be explained as three worlds. There is the *Uku Pacha*, or the Underground world. There is the *Kay Pacha* or Middle World of this reality, and the *Hanan Pacha*, or the Upper World of the Light Beings.

## PachaKuti

In the Inca language, means "Return to the Essence of the Cosmos." We are entering a 500-year daytime of a 1000-year cosmic cycle.

## Pachamama

Our name for our beloved Mother Earth.

## paq'o

Quechua name for a priest who can perform ceremonies.

## quinua

An important high protein-grain.

## sami

Refined light energy that assists in reaching higher levels of consciousness.

**sonccoqui**

The ever-flowing joy and abundance that manifests in our lives when we reach the higher levels of the third Inca Law of Yachay, Wisdom.

**Taripay Pacha**

A saying in Quechua that means "time to find yourself." This time is now.

**Tayta Inti**

The name for the Father Sun.

**totora**

A reed that grows in Lake Titicaca and supplies the Uros community with food, shelter, fuel, and material for boats. The Uros live on islands built on the roots of the reeds.

**tucuy llancayniyoc**

The more advanced practice of Llancay, work or service.

**tucuy munayniyoc**

The more advanced practice of Munay, love.

**tucuy yachayniyoc**

The more advanced practice of Yachay, wisdom.

**tupananchiscama**

An expression that means "until I encounter you again." This meeting can be in any reality.

**Waira**

Quechua word for the wind.

**wifala**

Pre-Incan flag with forty-nine squares of the rainbow colors.

**Yachay**

Third Inca Law. It is the Law of Wisdom in which you connect with your inner spiritual or authentic self.

**yatiri**

Aymara word for an Andean priest who can perform ceremonies, or a spiritual leader.

# INDEX

Acora, 45

Akamari, 169

Alejandro, 6–7, 15

Amantani Island, 34, 108–109, 112–
114, 140

Antonio, 50–64

apacheta, 75, 110, 155

Apukunas, 51, 59, 66, 73, 103, 105,
126, 137

Apu(s), 3, 7, 22, 29, 44, 54–55, 60, 68,
73–75, 77–79, 105, 116–117, 120,
122–123, 127, 130, 133,135, 138,
147–148, 155

Aguas Calientes, 146, 160

Arequipa, 24–25

Aramu Muru, 3, 15–16, 46

Aramu Muru's Doorway (Doorway),
3, 5, 14–17, 46

Ausangate Mountain, 66, 68, 76–77

Aymara, 2, 6, 9–10, 17, 19–21, 26, 29,
31, 41, 56, 61, 107

ayni, 16, 59, 158

Bebedero del Inca, 11–12

callawaya, 116–117, 120–121, 123–
125, 127

Cederño, Ruben, 44–46

chacana, 39, 131, 135, 137

chacaruna, 16–17, 64, 79–80, 127, 167

chakra, 73

challa, 63, 126

Charazani, 115–118, 123, 125–126

chicha, 11–12, 57, 59, 76, 78, 119, 134

Chilca, 37

Children of the Sun, 2–3, 15–16,
58–59, 106–107, 140, 147, 149–150,
155, 158, 165, 167

chincana(s), 110–112

cholla, (o), 21–22

chullpa(s), 37–39, 100–103, 106,–107

condor, 13, 55, 59–61, 73, 77, 106,
118, 120–122, 133, 135–138, 149,
154–155

Condori, 45–46

conopas, 27, 76

Copamaya, 7–9, 11

Cutimbo, 101–102, 105–107

crystal, 17, 27, 31, 33–38, 40, 47, 55,
57, 76, 113, 142, 160

Crystal City, 6, 132, 155, 164–165

Cusco, 6, 23, 36–38, 45–46, 66–68, 109,
112, 132, 140–142, 165

cuyas, 27, 76

Daniel, 118, 120–127

despacho, 54, 62–63, 66, 74, 76, 78–79,
116–117, 120–125

Ruiz, Miguel, 132–139, 142–144

Father Sun, 2, 4, 7–8, 12, 29, 39, 50,
105, 107, 140, 150–151

Five Kingdoms, 105

Golden Disc, 6, 15, 46, 141

Hanan Pacha, 55, 58–59, 61, 148.

Hatun Inti, 15, 147, 156, 165

hucha, 102, 136

Ichu, 6–7

Illampu, 7, 12, 169

illas, 27

Inti, 8, 107, 132, 146–148, 150–151,
164

Juliaca, 23, 30, 40, 44

kantuta, 8

kawsay, 140

Kay Pacha, 55, 57–58, 132, 140, 143,
148

kintui, 12, 55–56, 79, 102–103, 111,
126, 133–134, 148

kontiki, 60–61

Lake Titicaca, 6, 8, 11, 15, 20, 23,
28–31, 34–35, 38, 40– 41, 43–46,
61, 100, 106, 112, 114, 117, 130,
140–141

Lake Umayu, 39

Lemuria, 15, 141

Le Paz, 45

ley line, 13–14, 30, 46 100, 109, 112,
140

Llancay, 78, 151, 154, 157–159,
161–164

Madonna, 23, 28, 109

Machu Picchu, 39, 45, 60, 77, 130, 132, 146–152, 154–157, 159–160, 162, 165, 169
Mama Coca, 11, 105–106, 123, 134, 149
Mama Cocha, 29, 76, 126
Mama Killa, 105, 131
Mama Ocllo, 29, 34, 140
Mama Sara, 11, 105, 108, 134
Mama Simona, 77, 169
Manco (Mallcu) Capac, 29, 34, 140
Mariano, 67–80
mesa, 27, 42, 74–78, 100–102, 111, 123, 125–127, 160
Moon (Luna) Island, 34, 141.
Moray, 138–139
Mother Earth, 2, 8, 10, 16, 28–29, 34, 39, 46, 50–51, 56–58, 62–63, 66–67, 75, 109, 111, 116, 126–127, 130, 132–135, 140, 148, 150–152, 154, 158, 161
Munay, 78, 150, 154, 157, 161–164
New Sunrise, 3–4, 15–16, 46, 58
Ollantaytambo, 61, 130–132, 137–138
Pacha, 55, 57, 59, 64, 66, 102, 136, 147, 150–153
PachaKuti, 3, 15–16, 58, 164.
Pachamama, 8, 28, 54, 56, 60, 63, 75, 77, 80, 102, 108, 110–111, 126, 133–134, 137, 147, 150–151, 154, 161, 164
paq'o, 51, 54–56, 62–63, 67, 73–74, 109, 111, 157
Paratia, 50–55, 57, 61, 71, 152
Pisac, 135–136
Pitusiray, 133, 169
Pucara, 7, 46
puma, 12–13, 29–30, 55, 58, 102–104, 106, 114, 133, 137, 140, 146
Puno, 6, 20–21, 23, 26, 28, 30–31, 37, 40–41, 50–52, 61, 67, 101, 106, 108–109, 112, 116, 123
Putu Cusi, 60, 77, 148, 169
Q'ero, 66–72, 75-76, 126, 144, 152, 157, 169
Quechua, 2, 6, 16, 21, 26, 29, 51, 56, 58, 66–67, 69–71, 108
quinua, 51, 56
Reed Islands, 34, 43–44, 109
Sacred Lake, 29–31, 34–35, 76, 100, 141
Sacred Valley, 37, 61, 100, 108, 129–130, 132, 138, 140
Salkantay, 169
sami, 103
Sawasiray, 133, 169
Shapero, Joshua , 113–114
Sillustani, 37–39
Silva, Natalio, 42–44
sonccoqui, 158
snake, 13, 55–56, 102, 106, 133–134, 148
Sun. See Falther Sun
Sun (Sol) Island, 12, 29, 34
Tapikala, 117, 140
Taripay Pacha, 58
Tayta Inti, 147
Taquile Island, 34–35, 38
Tiawanaku, 7, 30, 46, 109–110, 140
Tipon, 142–143
totora, 43
tucuy llancayniyoc, 151
tucuy munayniyoc, 150
tucuy yachayniyoc, 152
Tunupa, 61, 130–131, 169
tupananchiscama, 67, 144
Urubamba, 130, 132, 138
Urubamba River, 130, 147
Urco, 133–134
Uros, 34, 43, 109
waira, 77, 110
Wakac Willka, 76, 169
Wayna Picchu, 77, 148, 169
wifala, 39
Yachay, 78, 152, 154, 157, 159, 161–162, 164
Yanantin, 138, 147, 169
yatiri, 6, 20, 31, 41–45, 50, 54, 61–62, 74, 100, 155, 157, 161

# About the Author

JORGE LUIS DELGADO, a modern Inca by birth and heritage, lives his beliefs. He firmly walks the spiritual path of the chacaruna, as well as the paths of husband, father, and businessman. In Inca tradition there is not a separation of the physical life and the spiritual life. His passion is to bring authentic Inca heritage, spiritual traditions and handicrafts to worldwide attention. Jorge Luis began his career as a tour guide when he finished his formal schooling in Puno, Peru. Since then, he has established a tour company, Kontiki Tours of Puno and Cusco. He has built several hotels in the areas of Lake Titicaca and Cusco. Jorge Luis considers the oral traditions, taught in the different Inca communities, as his ever-expanding higher education. He is a collector and expert in the artifacts and handicrafts of the Inca people. Jorge Luis invites everyone to claim our common heritage as Children of the Sun and experience, by book or in person, the true Inca spirit at the very alive and vital Inca sites in Peru.

Jorge's travel agency is Kontiki Tours E.I.R.L.
www.kontiki@kontikiperu.com; reservas@kontikiperu.com

For more recent information about Jorge Luis Delgado and his work, see www.andeanawakening.com.

MARYANN MALE, PHD met Jorge Luis when she and her husband, Theron, traveled to Peru. They were so taken with Jorge Luis and the spiritual traditions of the Incas that they returned to journey with Jorge Luis to meet his teachers. During this time they asked Jorge Luis to bring his authentic voice to the world via a book. MaryAnn and Theron returned many times to study with Jorge Luis and are proud to have him as their mentor and friend. MaryAnn and Theron reside near Philadelphia, PA, close to their children and grandchildren.